Melba Maggay has written an enthralling account word of God can be applied creatively to many of tł confronting the modern world. Taking some of th that speak of God's acts of creation, the consequences of humanity's rejection of God, God's plan for a new community of people restored to fellowship, and the final end of history, she shows imaginatively just how contemporary the whole biblical story proves itself to be. She is sure in her grasp of the historical and linguistic background to the text, relating it constantly to its own context. Melba has a most engaging style of writing, with many arresting turns of phrase. The result is a book whose (often poetic) prose is a delight to read. Readers will find this a refreshingly novel, inventive and compelling demonstration of the art of communicating to a thoroughly perplexed generation, across cultures and nations, the biblical explanation of human reality.

Dr J. Andrew Kirk
Senior Research Fellow, International Baptist Theological Study Centre, Amsterdam

Global Kingdom, Global People is a brilliant book capturing well the author's experience in a place of pain; this is tough research and honest reflection on a biblical theme and perspective. It draws the reader to seriously consider a personal and collective response to contemporary global missional challenges.

CB Samuel
Theological Advisor
The Evangelical Fellowship of India Commission on Relief (EFICOR), India

Global Kingdom, Global People is a sweeping, probing reflection on what it means to follow Christ in our day by a senior evangelical missiologist who reads very widely and writes brilliantly. Thoroughly immersed in her local setting in the Phillipines, Dr Maggay illuminates and critiques the way globalization works today, combining a creative analysis of a broad sweep of biblical texts with contemporary socio-economic analysis. An important voice.

Ronald J. Sider
Senior Distinguished Professor of Theology, Holistic Ministry, and Public Policy
Palmer Seminary at Eastern University, Pennsylvania, USA

Global Kingdom, Global People is a splendid little book full of insight into, and cogent reflection on, Scripture and full of conviction and compassion. Countless works have been written on the themes of culture, globalization and mission; the most jaded literary palate will find something fresh and interesting or inspiring from this one and not least from the illuminating comments from Melba Maggay's Philippine context.

Andrew F. Walls
University of Edinburgh, Liverpool Hope University
and Akrofi-Christaller Institute, Ghana

Melba Maggay offers us a penetrating interweaving of the biblical text with key issues of our contemporary world. Academically rigorous, and authoritative in its sweep, the book offers us a cosmic grasp of history, while remaining contemporary and relevant in its application to our world today. She opens up the biblical story with flair and imagination, bringing the themes of mission, globalization and culture alive in a fresh and detailed way. Her breadth of scholarship peppers the text with insights, exposing cultural myths and inviting her readers into a more thoughtful Christian perspective. The result is a crucially important book, written through the experience and reflections of a very fine writer.

Elaine Storkey
Former President of Tearfund

As we have come to expect from Melba Maggay, she gives us not just political dreams or ready answers but her own journey of engaging the stark realities of the real world of human beings and her own honest grappling with real issues and struggles therein. Such issues would not just leave us alone to chart our own Christian course. Christ's followers remain on earth not merely to build our own programme, structures, mission or institutions in self-isolation, but to do so in relevant and effective conversation and engagement with the rest of humanity. Today's followers of Christ must not just *live faithfully* but to do so with understanding and informed consideration for a *multicultural world*.

GOH Keat Peng
Honorary Vice-President of IFES
Former Head of World Vision Malaysia
Activist and Campaigner

Global Kingdom,
Global People

With warm
appreciation

Langham
GLOBAL LIBRARY

Global Kingdom, Global People

Living Faithfully in a Multicultural World

Melba Padilla Maggay

Published 2017 by Langham Global Library
An imprint of Langham Creative Projects

Langham Partnership
PO Box 296, Carlisle, Cumbria CA3 9WZ, UK
www.langham.org

ISBNs:
978-1-78368-198-3 Print
978-1-78368-200-3 Mobi
978-1-78368-199-0 ePub
978-1-78368-201-0 PDF

British Library Cataloguing in Publication Data
A catalogue record for this book is available from the British Library

ISBN: 978-1-78368-198-3

Cover & Book Design: projectluz.com

CONTENTS

Foreword

Love Is Local

On the northernmost tip of Palawan, the westernmost island in the Philippines, lies the community of El Nido, "The Nest." It is so named because the birds' nests used in Chinese soups are harvested from the high limestone cliffs nearby. Besides scrounging for nests, the people of El Nido work in subsistence farming and fishing, or in a series of tour guide businesses crammed cheek-by-jowl along the main street. There is an NGO that serves as an ecological center. That nature conservancy protects marine resources and teaches sustainable gardening and animal husbandry, marketing of produce and crafts, and family planning.

El Nido is part of Melba Maggay's story. In the latter half of the nineteenth century, Melba's mestizo gentry ancestors settled in Palawan, where they nurtured genteel values on the edge of its wild timberland and coastal richness. Some of them still speak the local indigenous language. Later, the family suffered the Japanese invasion and incarceration of Melba's father. During those war years, Melba's mother with her then six children (she would eventually have a dozen) made and sold rice cakes to survive and brought eggs to famished *kempetai* soldiers as bribes in exchange for jail visits. Today, Melba and all her siblings own plots of land on this island. Someday she may build a bed-and-breakfast there, but for now her land is planted in trees.

When I was in Palawan, Melba and I took a day-long boat ride to multiple islets, swam in the bobbing waves, enjoyed fruit and fresh-caught fish grilled on the beach, and in the evening sang hymns to an outrageously out-of-tune piano. Green was everywhere, in the rice fields and in the thousands of coconut palms swaying gracefully. Dozens of big brown water buffalos with great curved horns munched grass and wallowed in mud holes. Serving as plow-and-truck-power for many a family, these animals were valued. Bamboo homes on stilts dotted the island, decorated by squares, diamonds, and zigzag patterns woven into the bamboo window shutters and veranda rails.

The town cemetery bordered the sea, a solid line of blue along the horizon. Old graves lurched and slanted toward the sandy soil. This was a venerable burial place, the kind where boat-of-the-dead motifs might still be found in the gravestones. As sea levels rise these crypts will be endangered. Yet Melba's sister was buried here last year, joining generations of family. A noted educator, this woman was honored by memorial services in several places throughout the province before coming to her final earthly rest beside the waves.

In this book, Melba argues that cultures matter. That might be disputed in an era of globalization. Emphasizing cultural distinctives might be viewed as regressive. Emphasizing ethnicity might even exacerbate violence and contribute to wars. Perhaps in our time cultural differences should be minimized. Perhaps cultures do not matter so much anymore.

Melba firmly disagrees with such views. God loves cultures, she asserts, and she rolls out support for her position from Genesis to Revelation. God delights in the particularities of the world that he has made. Not only the dazzling variety of the natural world honors him. The kaleidoscope of diverse human communities with their contrasting patterns and heritages glorifies God too. Cultures do contain sin. God judges them. However, this does not obliterate the gifts of God's common grace in our societies, the results of humans expressing their God-given creativity. This is not abstract theology for Melba. It begins in the families and fields and waters of Palawan where she was raised as a child to love nature and society. That is her experience as well as her doctrine. When she stirs squid with onions and garlic and oil, patiently participating in the rhythms of cooking, she glorifies God, just as when she exercises what she calls her "prophetic imagination" to birth books.

In this volume, Melba argues that while cultures are to be affirmed, they are not pristine units separate from one another. Certainly in the twenty-first century, when 200 million people live outside the countries where they were born, cultures are interwoven in a complex way, one with another. Filipinos constitute a significant part of the global diaspora. The Philippine economy is so constructed that more than ten per cent of the population must work overseas and send remittances back to their family members. Melba explores this inescapable reality.

Throughout the book, Melba also discusses justice. This has long been a priority for her. As a Marxist-leaning university student, Melba discovered to her surprise that the gospel condemned perversion of justice and exploitation of the vulnerable. It affirmed humane work conditions, loyal rather than transactional commitments between employers and employees, and embodied stewardship rather than absentee relations between land and people. During the peaceful People Power Revolution that ousted President Marcos, Melba led the evangelical presence in the barricades when at great risk the people faced the tanks and guns of the regime. Since the devastating tsunami in the Central Philippines, she has led professional teams devoting thousands of hours to doing trauma care and creative therapy for the shattered communities there.

On the global scene, Melba accompanies many faith-based development organizations as president of Micah Global, a network of more than 700 organizations working among the poor worldwide. Originally known as the Micah Network, it spawned the Micah Challenge, a campaign for achieving the United Nations' Millenium Development Goals. Micah Global is part of the World Evangelical Alliance, a fellowship of Christians in more than 120 countries.

Infused with justice themes, this book is particularly concerned about the ease with which multinational businesses and powerful foreign interests squelch national and indigenous efforts.

The book concludes with the great party described in Revelation 7, which welcomes representatives from every nation, tribe, people, and language. Melba writes:

> We are not immune from calamities. We reel from earthquakes. We are buffeted by wind and waves in deadly typhoons. Crops suffer drought. Sea creatures become inedible through red tide. Teeming settlers precariously perched along waterways become both cause and victim of environmental disasters.
>
> The experience of disaster and social devastation is universal. Human solidarity is such that we all suffer hardships and political turmoil.
>
> What we *are* sealed from is the awful judgment of God upon sinful humanity at the close of history. In contrast, at the heart of John's vision are the people of God made safe and secure and joyfully at worship. More than all other occupations, worship decenters our attention from the terrible instability and fearfulness of life, and re-centers our vision on him "who sits upon the throne." We are reminded that "salvation belongs to our God," and it is he who sits at the center of all power.

It would be a great pain not to be part of this joyous, multi-cultural throng. Those of us who come from cultures whose main idea of joy is sitting around at table with family, relatives and friends in a great fiesta would feel the loss keenly if we found ourselves excluded from the Great Banquet prepared by the Lamb.

Melba was her mother's ninth child. It was a crisis pregnancy. Many years later, her mother told her that she was then so sick she could hardly comb her hair without feeling tired. She was advised to have an abortion as she could lose her life along with the baby. "The doctors stood solemnly in a row and looked at me with sorrow in their eyes. They wanted you out of me. They gave me little pills to swallow so you would come out as a little clot of blood." But then her mother and father prayed, and told the doctors, "We will trust God for this child." Her mother gathered her in her ample arms and said, "We have always loved you, child, even then."

That is the kind of love that flows through this book: God's love expressed in very concrete and problematic situations in God's world.

Miriam Adeney, PhD
Seattle Pacific University, 2016

Introduction

The Way We Live Now

We live in a global age, a time of great mobility, when masses of people cross borders out of curiosity, economic necessity or social disintegration. Mass travel, migration and the flight of refugees from war-torn regions has made us all come together in megasocieties.

Living in racially mixed and polyglot societies has caused the problem of integration to surface. How do we live with a stranger who has become our neighbor? What happens when cultures and peoples are thrown together? How do we move among a people whose way of life is not our own and stretches our comfort zones?

Much literature has emerged posing penetrating analyses and critiques of globalization and its impact on all that is happening in the world today.[1] It is not our intention to repeat the themes and tensions that have been surfaced. Our present task is simply to sharpen the questions already put forward by framing them in the light of Scripture. The following biblical reflections are a groping effort to struggle for insight in a time when we lack even the language to name what is before us.

In particular, we seek to address the following issues:

Primal Identities and the Challenge of Multiculturalism

One cluster of questions has to do with the rise of "primal identities," now that we are face to face and crowding out each other's space. It would seem that while we are witnessing unprecedented levels of global integration in the economic sphere, we are also seeing the disintegration of nation states.

---

1. An early critique was *The Case against the Global Economy, and a Turn toward the Local*, a compendium edited by Jerry Mander and Edward Goldsmith (San Francisco, CA: Sierra Club Books, 1996).

The "Arab Spring" has turned into a bitter winter of discontent for millions in Syria and other fragile states in the Middle East. Fratricidal wars have intensified in many pockets of conflict in the world, whether impelled by "ethnic cleansing" as with Bosnia and the Balkan states or fueled by ancient grievance as with our Muslims in the South or the Basques in Spain. Tribal wars now and again erupt as with the Hutus and Tutsis in Rwanda, exacerbated by religious undercurrents as with Nigeria or the Syrian civil war. These, together with the rise of militant political religions as represented by the ISIS or, in a more civil and civic form, the Religious Right in the US, has put at center stage the reassertion of more primitive identities, usually ethnically or religiously defined.

Clearly, there is a centripetal movement towards economic integration. But there is also a centrifugal movement towards political anomie and disintegration.

The reasons behind this fragmentation are complex and many.

One reason is historical: the imposition of national boundaries that have little to do with the realities of indigenous tribal groupings. Africa used to have at least two thousand ethnic units that in the age of imperialism were clustered into half a dozen colonial blocs controlled from six European capitals. In the aftermath of post-colonial rearrangements, these were broken up into small nation-states that crisscrossed tribal lines, creating a volatile underside of minorities that tended to get marginalized by the majority tribe in power. With some variations on the same theme, the many hot spots of conflict in various regions are often wars of grievance, or wars of self-determination waged by those in the periphery against those in the centers of power.

Another reason is correlative to the first: the collapse of belief in great architectonic systems based on ideology or the artificially-imposed construct of a "nation-state." With the failure of the Marxist social experiment in iron curtain countries and the bad experience of centralized governance by corrupt elites, countries in the poorer world went through a crisis of paradigm. In the effort to cast about for some coherent social glue by which to cobble together warring tribes and ethnicities, many are returning and falling back on the resources of their cultures and faith traditions. With the onslaught of homogenizing forces brought about by globalization, this movement towards a reinvented indigeneity has morphed into a virtual jihad against McWorld and all that threatens people's identities.

In global centers, the postmodern rejection of grand narratives – whether political, religious or ideological – held out the exciting promise of diversity. In recent years, however, this has transmogrified into pressures to legislate cultural conformity and fears for homeland security. Vinoth Ramachandra, writing on global myths, has remarked that "the irony of current technological and economic changes is that, while globalization and the idea of a global village are being constantly touted, national borders in rich nations have been vigorously reasserted and fortified to keep out refugees and undesirable immigrants."[2] The European indifference to the thousands who flee from rouge states and drown in the desperate attempt to reach the shores of Lampedusa in Italy is a mute witness to this.

How do we face up to the challenges of migration and the pressures they put on the social safety and economic resilience of host nations? How do we live together as a community in a world where strange neighbors have invaded our living space and do not abide by the usual rules and traditions in which we have been raised? How do we remain faithful to our Christian faith within a plurality of religions? How do we make sense of our faith in various cultural contexts?

The Myth of a Global Redistribution of Wealth

Another set of questions we have to face is the massive exclusion of the poor from the wealth generated by today's global technologies and productive processes. Asia has been a net gainer in the shifts in global wealth. However, it is estimated that fully two-thirds of Asia and of the world's populations are being excluded from the "global middle class" that is rising from the emergent markets of Asia, Latin America and Eastern Europe. From the giddy sense that there is a "brave new world" out there, things have begun to look like a "slave new world."

Decades ago, I was asked to speak at an urban conference titled "Writing the History of the Future" in an American college.[3] The title struck me as historically optimistic. It assumed that there is a probable future that can be imagined from the present. The future is one that we can desire and shape by

---

2. Vinoth Ramachandra, *Subverting Global Myths, Theology and the Public Issues Shaping Our World* (Downers Grove, IL: InterVarsity, 2008), 113.

3. Some of my remarks in this book were made in that original address at the Claremont Urban Convocation, "Writing the History of the Future," 31 October – 2 November 2000, Claremont College, CA, USA.

our ideals and our ability to invent technologies and programs that will get us there. As the old saying went, "We may not know exactly where we are going, but we are on our way."

This confidence struck me as peculiarly American. Other cultures are stuck with the past. Most traditional societies believe that history goes in cycles and repeats itself. Old empires where the sun has set often make you feel that everything glorious is in the past. Some other cultures, like the Filipino culture, are mostly focused on the present, preoccupied with the exigencies of survival and unwilling to spend time and energy trying to manage a future that is seen as at best quirky, and at any rate is usually unpredictable and beyond control.

The USA, in contrast, always dreams of a future. Since the pilgrim fathers fled the decaying monarchies of Europe, it has always staked itself on the viability of its social vision, with a confidence that seems to me to be a curious mix of the rugged faith of the Puritan and a rough-and-ready entrepreneurial spirit that at its best is seen in the frontiersman and at its worst is embodied in the hard opportunism of the carpetbagger. The vastness of its land allowed the sense that one can always go "out West" and begin again, without the encumbrance of tradition or memory.

In the 1990s there was a similar sense that the human race is standing at the threshold of a new frontier, before the limitless possibilities of information technologies and the open-ended future that it holds. Among its pioneers, there was the feeling of being like Christopher Columbus, sailing a vast, "open sea" as Nietzche once put it, with an ever-receding horizon, a place where the boundaries move and the old rules don't apply.

At first instance, this heady sense of adventure sourced its optimism from the notion that deregulated market forces and creative technologies will combine to liberate societies from economic inefficiencies and political autocracies. We no longer need to worry about the poor; we just need to get them outfitted for survival in the market as micro-entrepreneurs. We no longer need to mount revolutions, nor, Cold-War style, stage destabilizing coups. Economic integration will soften despots and turn recalcitrant regimes into emerging democracies. Technology and the market will fix it. Together they will deliver us from the long-standing ills that plague societies, especially those fractured, pre-modern ones that are perennial basket cases.

Globalization as an economic process was once heralded as a rising tide that will "lift all boats." So far, it has mostly inaugurated an era of unprecedented disparity in wealth and opportunity within and among nations. As an American radio talk show host describes it in plain speaking: "A rising tide lifts all boats, but if you're in a yacht and I'm in a dinghy, we still got a problem here. And that's not counting the folks who are in the water but don't have a yacht or a dinghy."[4]

From where I sit, the gap between rich and poor has risen to horrendous proportions. In the city where I live, our professional elite is cocooned in luxury condominiums set in modern townships that look like transplanted mini-cities copied from somewhere else. They run around town with BMWs and smart phones while more than half the population are in squatter settlements with no potable water. With rural lands turned into export crops and golf courses, the poor mass around our cities and prefer to live precariously along waterways and on garbage heaps and suffer conditions that are far more degrading than those they left behind.

This is partly due to an uncritical acceptance of the ruling paradigm of "development," understood as a linear, incremental advance towards higher and higher stages of economic and technological growth that filters down to the poor. For half a century this has proved to be inadequate in dealing with long-standing social imbalances and the gross distortions brought about by the rapid and uneven diffusion of modernizing forces and lifestyles. It is a wonder this has persisted as a dominant theory in going about the business of lifting the poor.[5]

It would seem that in more liberal societies, there is a ready sense of pluralism when it comes to the softer aspects of organizing our common life. We are careful to be inclusive, to give public space to minorities of all sorts, whatever the ethnic origin, religious orientation, sexual preference and other such issues touching alternative lifestyles.

However, such broad tolerance concerns matters that in truth are peripheral to shaping social organization. There is nothing pluralistic about the hegemony of the market as the center of today's organized life. We only need to ask those high-powered techies of Silicon Valley just how much their lives are organized round serving the altar of global competitiveness.

Where is the kingdom in all this? What is the shape of our missional engagement in the face of the powers as expressed in the dominance of the market and technology as singular forces shaping our lives today?

---

4. Tavis Smiley, quoted in "On the Future of Capitalism," *Time Magazine*, 25 May 2009.

5. For a more extended discussion of this please see the first three chapters of the author's *Rise Up and Walk: Religion and Culture in Empowering the Poor* (Oxford: Regnum and the Oxford Center for Mission Studies, 2015).

Global Dreams and the Global Church

A peculiar feature of the way we live now is the rather bizarre presence of sophisticated technologies in places of deprivation, as with our teenagers in the slums who spend all their time texting each other on expensive cell phones. Goods that serve the elaborate needs of slick elites in high-consumption societies can be found in crowded and chaotic cities like Manila where the life system is such that pollution kills you softly and traffic rules are only suggestions. As has been observed a while back, "An African village could juxtapose some of the signs of pre-modern, modern and postmodern lives in a single space, encompassing the plough, the automobile, Coca Cola and Madonna's songs and semi-nude pictures."[6]

Through global media, our people are exposed to rising levels of wants while at the same time trapped in misery. These rising expectations can be a threat to political safety. Poverty is not bearable when media floods us with images of fabulous wealth, and the glitzy lives of the rich somehow make us feel diminished.

How do we bear witness to the lordship of Jesus in a world where our dreams and our very imagination dances to the tune of the siren call of consumerism? How do we arrest attention in a crowded marketplace where media dominates and has become the arbiter of what gets into public space?

Part of the crisis of today's nation-states is the breakdown of a common cultural meaning which used to be rooted in their old religious traditions.

How does a nation preserve its cherished values and spiritual tradition while at the same time remaining friendly to people of another religious orientation? How do we live together as diverse peoples in societies no longer bound by a common faith tradition?

There are voices telling us to go back to the old civilizational comforts of "Christendom," or quixotically reconstruct a "cultural consensus" based on the nostalgic idea of a "Christian society." That churches are being turned into pubs is a sad consequence of the failure to engage the secular imagination at a level that speaks to its soul, beyond the usual furniture of religion, and down to those depths that long for meaning and purpose and coherence even when it has surrendered the possibility that the scattered bits and pieces of one's life can be put together.

---

6. See the essay of Majid Tehranian and Katharine Kia, "That Recurrent Suspicion: Democratization in a Global Perspective," in *The Democratization of Communication*, ed. Philip Lee (Cardiff: University of Wales Press, 1995).

That some of the world's largest mosques and Buddhist temples are now in Europe is an indication that there is a resurgence of spirituality, but of a kind that is outside the "Christian culture" of the West. It is more at home within the more intuitive, meditational and therapeutic rites of Eastern religions.

The world, indeed, has pluralized in ways that drive us to search Scriptures anew for some compass by which we can navigate the tortuous waters swirling around us. Churches in the North and their offshoots in the South are faced with the challenge of riding the waves and making sense of their faith in a vastly different context. We hope the following biblical reflections will lead us to finding our way through the open sea.

Part I

The Roots of Culture

1

Revisiting the Cultural Mandate

Then God said, "Let us make man in our image, after our likeness;
and let them have dominion . . . So God created man in his own
image, in the image of God he created him; male and female he
created them. And God blessed them, and God said to them, "Be
fruitful and multiply, and fill the earth and subdue it; and have
dominion over the fish of the sea and over the birds of the air and over
every living thing that moves upon the earth."

Genesis 1:26–28

Even in caves they painted. Already, when it was yet dark and the world slept formless in the shadows, hands were feeling out forms and trying out colors.

By the light of the fire they told stories. Long, long stories about the parting of the land from the sea, the making of their fathers and the wind and the rain and the piling of hills and mountains. In that little circle of light, surrounded by darkness, the faces of the young and the old, men and women, glowed in the fire of words as deep as the silence and clutched at the heart as tenderly.

Much later, when the world has been defaced and heartbreaking pictures made of it, the artists still long for purity of form, for the hidden order that lies beneath the mangled guitar, the broken moon, the shattered, ugly faces.

Inside the humless, gleaming machine in which much of our lives are now lived, there is a longing for poetry, a hunger for the piercing, haunting song breaking softly through the deep and open vastness of a cold blue sky.

Whence comes this ancient ache for form and textures, for the flash of sunlight and the fine grain of sand? From where the well of words, the swell of rhyme, the drunken exultation of a song and the fever of a dance? What is it about us which lies behind the breathless curiosity for the secrets of nature and the joy of discovery? Why strive to conquer the sky and embrace the wide earth? Why the groping and melancholy longing for height and depth, the feel for the throbbing, inner life just beneath a leaf or a tree?

Imaging God

Long ago, we are told, the Lord God had a council within the godhead or among what appears to be his royal court[1] and decided to make humans. In his image he made them, male and female he created them (Gen 1:27).

This "image" has been variously interpreted as humans having rational powers, or physical and spiritual qualities resembling that of God, like the capacity for beauty and righteousness. More to the point, much of this "image" may have to do, first, with the ability to have "dominion" over creation, and being "male" and "female," as these descriptions follow immediately the idea and the act of creating humans.

"Let us make man in our image," God says, "and let them have dominion over the fish of the sea, and over the birds of the air, and over the cattle, and over all the earth, and over every creeping thing that creeps upon the earth." The first humans are to be tasked and equipped with all that it takes to govern all of creation.

Also, the "image" may mean, alongside the exercise of dominion, the instinct for communion, or the longing for community. We are made to exercise stewardship over the earth together, and to be in relationship with one another. Both are parts of our "personhood," or what makes us who we are – human.

To fully "image God," we are to be creatively at work, ordering creation in such a way that new things are made out of the earth and its riches, harnessing wind and rain and sea for the flourishing of both humans and the creatures in

---

1. The plural, "Let **us** make . . ." could be, according to scholars, (1) royal plural – God thinks aloud as "Elohim," which is grammatically plural, and may be our equivalent of "Your Royal Highness"; note that in our language we also shift to the plural "*kayo*" instead of "*ikaw*" when addressing eminent people out of respect; (2) a reference to the Trinity – which may be remote and anachronistic, as the Old Testament writer has yet no conception of the doctrine of the Trinity; (3) a divine council – referring to the governing assembly of angelic beings that supervise the world, which is most likely, according to recent scholarship. Cf. the use of "sons of God" in Job 1–2, which implies that the "image of God" is common to God and angels. See Barry L. Bandstra, *Reading the Old Testament: An Introduction to the Hebrew Bible*, 2nd ed. (Belmont, CA: Wadsworth, 1999), 59.

it. In making the world so, there has to be an element both of "maleness" and "femaleness," however these are defined in a given culture.

And so God blessed Adam and Eve, and gave them the capacity both to reproduce and produce. "Be fruitful and multiply, fill the earth and subdue it" (Gen 1:28). While this mandate to be fruitful refers primarily to increasing the population when the wide world had only two inhabitants, it also means that we are to grow, spread ourselves – "fill the earth" – and put our stamp on creation.

There is much to recommend the idea that the "image" refers not so much to what we "have," but to what we "do." It is a royal concept borrowed from the practice of erecting statues in conquered territories to represent Mesopotamian monarchs. The statue serves as a local representation of the deified distant ruler.[2] *Adam* (at this point still the generic and undifferentiated "human") is God's representative, as it were, to rule on earth.

This task is known in theology as the "cultural mandate." It is both a capacity and a command. Cultivating the earth – what we call "culture" – is our human contribution to creation, which was given to us in the raw. It is both the instinct and the ability to create and "subdue," to put form and symmetry to what otherwise would be a wild vastness.

Human beings are to imitate the Maker in his making. In the same way that God formed the earth out of the *tohu* (the Hebrew word for chaos or formless waste), and filled the bohu (the empty space or void) with sun and moon and living creatures on earth and sky, humans are to put shape to the tangle of growth and produce a profusion of goodly things out of the virgin earth.

Notice that the mandate has two sides – **growth** and **governance**. We are to multiply, but also to govern. This fact is often glossed over.

Side by side with the command to be **fruitful** is the command to **rule** over all of creation. The Hebrew words used for "dominion" or "rule" denote great effort; *radah* in verse 26 means to "trample," and *kabas* in verse 28 means to "tread down." Governance over creation is not without strenuous exertion; it requires work, even before the fall.

---

2. E. M. Curtis, "Images in Mesopotamia and the Bible: A Comparative Study," in *The Bible in the Light of Cuneiform Literature. Scripture in Context III,* Ancient Near Eastern Texts and Studies, eds. W. W. Hallo, B. W. Jones, and G. L. Mattingly (Lewiston, NY: Edwin Mellen, 1990), 60.

Growth and governance are meant to go together. Whether we are talking families, social systems or business, we can only grow to the extent that we are able to manage and sustain that growth.

The Mandate for Our Time

The collapse of socialist systems has resurfaced with fresh cogency the idea that any system that stifles individual initiative in growing the economy shall fail. Likewise, restrictive policies in many countries that severely curtail birthing and grossly allow abortion has led not only to the greying of those societies but also to the increasing unsustainability of their economies.

On the other hand, runaway growth, whether in population or in the burgeoning of cities and the expansion of economies, tends to violate the earth and its carrying capacity. Before the Bruntland Report, the Club of Rome in the 1960s had long issued an early warning that there are limits to growth. These days, disasters of unprecedented destructiveness now threaten us with devastating regularity, the result of rapacity and unbridled exploitation of the resources of the earth.

Growth and *governance* are twin principles we need to keep in mind in a time when our ecological system is in dire crisis, and global media and the market have become forces that shape the imagination of peoples and overrule the sovereignty of nations.

Whether we are aware of it or not, we now live in a secondary environment of mostly virtual realities conjured by media and market forces. Whether in the world of economics and finance or of culture and the arts, technology has made possible the wiring of the world in such a way that not only are we interconnected, but are shaped by what Jacques Ellul calls "shadows," phantoms in the imagination that make us captive to the seductions of the market and dream merchants that hide behind the anonymous authority of newspaper offices.

We may be in an age that is self-assertively autonomous, two hundred years after Friedrich Nietzche announced the "death of God" in western societies. In a globalizing world, we may be those who feel a certain power in being able to trumpet our opinions and ideological wares in social media. But the truth is much of our psychological and mental furniture is now shaped, not by the ground-level reality we experience – what C. S. Lewis called our "primal history" – but by technology and the market. These have now replaced the institutions of church and state as defining forces in our public life.

More than half a century after decolonization, the Philippines, like much of the Majority World, is in the throes of birthing a stable and prosperous nation. In the 1990s, there was optimism that globalization would "lift all boats." The resurgence of neo-liberal economies in the wake of the collapse of socialist states fueled the hope of a rising "global middle class" among poorer nations.

But the result so far has been massive inequality and intensifying poverty among the underclasses in both developed and emerging economies such as ours.

What has happened?

The factors behind all this are many and complex. Sociologists account this to the imbalances that have arisen in the wake of globalization. It is also easy to blame false ideologies, politics, our colonial history and its residual influence in our social and economic life. More productive is facing up to our own failure to properly grow and govern this country.

Unlike many places of scarcity in other parts of the world, the Philippines has no reason to be poor. Development theorists account the poverty of nations to certain "deficits" – lack of natural resources, lack of financial capital, lack of technology, or lack of an educated human capital. We have none of these deficits.

One glaring "deficit," however, is bad governance. Our rich resources get frittered away by mismanagement and the consequent inability to implement systems and structures that work. While the rules and laws are many, we are unable to level the playing field for productivity, or effectively curb such things as our runaway population growth and the systemic, unbridled greed that lies behind our corruption scandals.

It is time we pay attention to what it really takes to pursue growth with equity, and within the limits that God has built into his creation. Instead of accounting the failure of our societies to merely historical and external factors like colonization or globalization, let us also critique our own social development patterns in the pursuit of growth, and weigh our own capacity for governing that growth.

2

Dominion and Communion

In the day that the Lord God made the earth and the heavens, when no plant of the field was yet in the earth and no herb of the field had yet sprung up . . . then the Lord God formed man of dust from the ground, and breathed into his nostrils the breath of life, and man became a living being . . . The Lord God took the man and put him in the garden of Eden to till it and keep it. . . . Then the Lord God said, "It is not good that the man should be alone; I will make him a helper fit for him."

Genesis 2:4–18

More Than a "Higher Animal"

In Genesis chapter 2, we are given a closer, telescopic view of the creation story, this time focused on the human being in relation to the newly-created landscape.[1]

The narrative begins with a description of the earth as barren, bereft of water. In this Yahwist account, water is not an enemy, as in the Priestly narrative, but "an assisting element in creation."[2] A river runs through Eden, which flows out into four main headwaters, two of which can be located in the Fertile Crescent, said to be the cradle of civilization – the Tigris and Euphrates Rivers.

---

1. "In chapter 1 man is the pinnacle of a pyramid, in chapter 2 the center of a circle." Gerhard von Rad, quoting Jac in *Genesis: A Commentary*, rev. ed. (Philadelphia, PA: The Westminster Press, 1972), 77.

2. Ibid., 76.

"For *P* [Priestly tradition], the chaos of floodwaters would be replaced by an organized cosmos; for *J* [Jahwist source], the chaos of barrenness would be replaced by a fruitful garden."[3]

There is a note of anticipation in the way the created heavens and the earth waited for God to send rain and form the first human. Both are creative forces, necessary elements in the growth of plants and herbs and the work of tending the garden that God had made.

The making of "the man," – *adam* – is distinct from the making of the rest of the created world in that this time, God "breathes" himself into a piece of clay, almost like an embrace, and it becomes a "living being" (Gen 2:7).

This "breath of life" is not to be understood as the "spirit" or the "soul," by which we normally distinguish people from animals. This "breath" only means life, as in Genesis 7:22, where it is used of both humans and animals. The expression a "living being" is used also for birds, fish, and animals, as in 1:20, 21, 24, 30.[4] As the OT scholar Gerhard von Rad puts it, "the 'breath' makes man a living creature, a distinction not between 'body' and 'soul' but between 'body' and 'life,' which springs directly from God."[5]

This has profound implications in the way we understand what is eternal about us. Usually, we think of a disembodied "soul" that persists when we die. It is a Greek habit of thought to see the "body" as the earthly, disintegrating part, and the "soul" as the immortal part. Hence, we think that "saving souls" is more important than investing in the flourishing of human culture.

Yet we know instinctively that the body is to be cared for and honored because it is, in an important sense, who we are: being fat or thin, ugly or pretty, is inextricably tied to our self-image and sense of identity. When someone dies, we dress up the body, mourn over it, and treat it as something sacred. At the same time, we sense that the body is not exactly the person that we know. We speak of it as the "remains," *yung labi*, or what was left of

---

3. "P" stands for the priestly tradition of OT narratives and "J" is the Jahwist source or the more anthropomorphic account. (The book will use Yahwist instead of Jahwist.) The quote is from Eugene H. Maly, "Genesis," in *The Jerome Biblical Commentary*, eds. Raymond E. Brown, Joseph A. Fitzmyer, Roland E. Murphy (Englewood Cliffs, NJ: Prentice-Hall, 1968), 12.

4. The process of making the human being was not sequential. It was not as if we were formed from dust first, and then given breath, but "By an act of divine omnipotence man arose from the dust; and in the same moment in which the dust, by virtue of creative omnipotence, shaped itself into a human form, it was pervaded by the divine breath of life, and became a living being, so that we cannot say the body was created earlier than the soul." C. F. Keil and F. Delitzsch, eds., *The Pentateuch Vol 1*, *Commentary on the Old Testament in Ten Volumes* (Grand Rapids, MI: Eerdmans, 1981), as translated from the German, 78–79.

5. Von Rad, *Genesis*, 77.

the person. Something vital, the thing that used to animate it and made it the person we love and will miss, is gone. The body and the soul, together, is really the person we know.

In our indigenous language, I am told, *kataowan* (body) is also our *kataohan* (soul, personality). This is close to the Hebrew sense that a person has not a soul or a body; he *is* soul, and he *is* body. This is why the Christian hope is bodily resurrection, not immortality. For the truer picture is that God "breathed" us into a whole, living person, someone whose personality is like his. This likeness enables us to create and commune with him in a relationship of intimacy that is quite unlike anything animals are capable of.

This is where the "image" lies, and the origin of the paradox that puzzled the German philosopher Friedrich Nietzche, who once said that "Man is an extreme piece of nature, an animal that makes promises, and answers for the future."

It is true that we are continuous with the rest of material creation. We are of the same stuff as a lump of clay, a shapeless mass of putty, like the mud that gets under your boots and is trodden underfoot. Dust we are, of a piece with earth, *adamah,* no higher than the rest of creation.

But something happened when God "breathed" into us, something utterly discontinuous with the soil from which we sprung. Embedded in our very being is something of his nature – "eternity in our hearts" – such that we long for what poets and philosophers call the "higher things." We are not merely complicated organisms, a vertebrate animal who happened to have a fine thumb. Quite untidily, we are a "mixed spirit," as C. S. Lewis put it.

This is why we do not just breed; we sing love songs and invent rituals that sacralize the powerful drive of the sexes towards each other. We do not just feed; we create exquisite cuisines, decorate a table with flowers and get together for a lavish fiesta. We do not just live and die; we stake our lives on a dream or some social cause and express our grief by elaborate funeral rites, building pyramids or a Taj Mahal to immortalize the memory of a dead king or a loved one.

We are strange creatures that are of a piece of the earth that we trample on, yet we behave as if we shall live forever, unaccountably haunted by a lost paradise and nostalgic for heaven.

Made for Work

Aside from highlighting our peculiar constitution, the *Yahwist* story tells us that the newly-formed human was put in the garden to "till it and to keep it" (Gen 2:15). It is in our very nature to want to work, to make something creative out of the earth, harness wind and rain and grow living things. Adam was put at the center of an abundant paradise not so much to earn his keep, for every lush green plant and fruit-bearing tree is already there for food.

Beyond the need for sustenance is the need for a vocation. Unemployment, or merely grubbing for a living as cyberslaves in our call centers, or getting trapped in the profit-driven frenzy of Wall Street, is not God's idea of how we are to spend our lives.

We were meant for work that is more than drudgery. My idea of heaven has always been that it is a place where we shall find work, and work that fits us perfectly. Imagine a world where everyone does something one would pay for the privilege of doing, something that takes the best of who and what we are and makes it into a gift for the world and a hymn of praise to the Maker. Imagine a job that lets you sing, as our fathers and mothers did when once they planted rice and hunched over the cooking fire with the sense that nature dances like a bean sprout and crackles like flames leaping about.

Some of us today have similar moments, times when work gets transfigured and it feels part of the great creative force remaking the world. In my case, there are moments when the computer races with the words that come out of somewhere deep and strong. Often, however, the words trickle like the drought in our faucets in the heat of summer.

Work after the fall often leaves us parched, dried up like a hollow well. It stoops the shoulders, greys the hair and snuffs out the light in our eyes. It marks us, like the grime under the nails and the gnarled, stubby toes of our mountain people.

Yet still, even in our condition, work is somehow redemptive. In a land that exports its people as "hewers of wood and drawers of water" for the rest of the world – along with fish, bananas and pineapples – it is a gift just to be able to earn one's bread, even if in blood, sweat and tears. This, at least, is cause for thanks. I imagine it is out of this sense of the good creation, of God's providential care in the midst of hardship and suffering, that the American Negro spirituals were forged, hymns rising out of the soul of those whose calloused hands worked the cotton fields and looked up to the sky for relief and hope.

We still have a feel for this sometimes, especially in traditional societies where life is organic and we tend to work and play at the same time. Unfortunately, modernization has sold us the idea that life and work do not mix: from 8 a.m. to 5 p.m. we must put our noses to the grindstone, and then perhaps we may pick up the remains of our day, or whatever is left of our energies, and try and get a life.

The longing for meaningful work has been mostly understood in recent times as a drive towards fulfillment or "self-actualization." More accurately, it is obedience to the way we were made. "We make still by the law by which we're made," says the novelist J. R. R. Tolkien. In the very structure of the universe and of who we are is the instinct for beauty, order and significance, hence the longing to apply ourselves in satisfying curiosity and discover the world – its forms, patterns and inner workings – and remake it according to the imagination given to us.

This side of Eden, some of our work carries the weight of glory in it, while other work is tainted or found to be unbearably lightweight, to be blown away like chaff, or at the end of time discovered to be tinder boxes, like wood or hay or stubble that goes up in smoke. Our deeds follow us, says Scripture. Whether good or evil, it marks the world. Such is the significance of human work.

Sovereignty or Solidarity?

There are suggestions that "naming" is an act of dominion, not just over the world, but over women. This is the interpretation given to Adam naming the woman (Gen 2:23). It is said that this naming is an "act of sovereignty," a sign of male headship that is creation-designed.

We need to remember that the first chapter is a counter-narrative to this. God's design was for both the man and the woman to steward and lead the creatures of the earth, not each other. They are both meant to be co-regents over creation, equal partners in the task of ruling the world.

Both were given the capacity to order and classify the world according to its "thingness" – the reality of what it is as God had made it. It is important to note that this is more than putting on a label. It is the conceptual task of finding a precise word for describing the birds of the air and the beasts of the field and all other living creatures. It is the ability to recognize and put into words the exact and unique properties of each item in the created order.[6]

Keil and Delitzsch suggest that this naming is "a deep and direct mental insight into the nature of the animals," which eventually led to the awareness that no one could be found as a "help of his like," in which as soon as he sees it, he may recognize himself.[7]

> The narrative shows the personality of Adam in contrast with the non- personal animals, and the divine act in bringing these creatures so definitely before the mind of Adam was with the view to stirring within him the desire for human and personal companionship.[8]

The making of the woman out of the rib of "the man" has been interpreted as legitimizing "male headship" or the subordination of women based on creational precedence. The Apostle Paul is usually summoned to lend credence to this view: "For man did not come from woman, but woman from man; neither was man created for woman, but woman for man" (1 Cor 11:8–9, NIV).

Conservative scholars like Hurley tend to read into this account the rights of primogeniture: "The firstborn inherited command of resources and the responsibilities of leadership in the home and in worship . . . Paul's appeal to the prior formation of Adam is an assertion that Adam's status as the oldest carried with it the leadership appropriate to the firstborn."[9]

However, this reading seems anachronistic; it projects retroactively a symbolic meaning culled from a much later cultural pattern. Further, the idea of "firstborn" is nowhere ascribed to Adam; it is Jesus who is described as the "first-born of all creation" (Col 1:15–18).

As the story goes, Adam was not even "first created" as Hurley later qualifies. That the woman was taken "out of" (ek) the man has about as much significance as the fact that "the man" was formed from out of the dust. Valerie

---

6. Cf. Von Rad: "The emphasis is placed not on the invention of words but on that inner appropriation by recognition and interpretation that takes place in language . . . language is seen not as a means of communication but as an intellectual capacity by means of which man brings conceptual order to his sphere of life" (Von Rad, *Genesis*, 83).

7. Keil and Delitzsch, *Pentateuch*, 86.

8. E. F. Kevan, "Genesis," in *The New Bible Commentary*, ed. F. Davidson (Leicester: IVP, 1965), 79.

9. See James Hurley's article on "1 Corinthians," in *Man and Woman in Biblical Perspective* (Leicester: IVP, 1981).

Griffiths, commenting on the controversy over the meaning of *kephale* or "head" in 1 Corinthians 11, takes issue with the idea of headship based on creational precedence:

> The woman was taken from the man, but the man was formed from dust already created, and his creation glorifies the Creator, not the dust. When woman was formed man was totally passive, asleep. God's direct purposeful act brought her into being. The method emphasized the common humanity which they share.[10]

More fundamentally, it needs noticing that when God said "it is not good for the man to be alone, I will make a helper suitable for him," (Gen 2:18, NIV) the Hebrew word used here for "the man" – *Adam* – is generic and collective, and refers not just to the one who will later become "man" but also to the latent "woman." It is not until verse 20b that the name "Adam" becomes a proper noun and refers to the sexually differentiated male.[11]

It is not good – for the woman no less than for the man – to be alone; they both need a "helpmate." Both were designed, when separated, to find self-completion in each other.

Unfortunately, the word "helpmate" or "helper" has connotations in this and other cultures of someone socially inferior, or at best, an assistant or a junior partner. It should be noted that the Old Testament use of the Hebrew word *ezer* mostly referred to God. Of the twenty-one times it was used, seventeen was in reference to God. As the Mennonite scholar Swartley notes, "If the word *ezer* is to be interpreted as an assistant of inferior status, this would contradict its constant use in the Old Testament."[12]

In this culture, it is more accurate to translate it as *katuwang* rather than *katulong*.

The joy of beholding someone like himself is underscored in Adam's thrice-repeated "this one" (also translated "she"): "This at last is bone of my bones, flesh of my flesh; she shall be called 'woman,' (Heb. *ishshah*), for she

---

10. Valerie Griffiths, "Mankind Male and Female," in *The Role of Women (When Christians Disagree)*, ed. Shirley Lees (Leicester: IVP, 1984), 74.

11. "Adam" at this point is "neither male, in the sense of complete sexual distinction, nor androgynous, as though both sexes were combined in the one individual created at the first, but as created in anticipation of the future, with a preponderant tendency, a male in simple potentiality, out of which state he passed, the moment the woman stood by his side, when the mere *potentia* became an actual antithesis" (Keil and Delitzsch, quoting Ziegler, *Pentateuch*, 88).

12. Willard Swartley, *Slavery, Sabbath, War and Women: Case Studies in Biblical Interpretations* (Scottdale, PA: Herald Press, 1983), 155.

was taken out of 'man' (Heb. *is*')" (Gen 2:23). In contrast to the animals, here is someone who wondrously mirrors his likeness.

Moreover, some scholars say that Adam here is not so much exercising his duty as name-giver, but as a lover singing and celebrating someone who is, finally, a match for him – he is *ish* and she is *ishshah*.[13] The emphasis is on the joyful recognition of similarity, of sameness, of having found a "soulmate."

Herein lies the mystery of human solidarity, of the sense of corporate identity and the longing for community. As we seek, behold and discover the "other" in all of her strangeness, we also recognize who we truly are. In acknowledging our shared humanity through all the differences – in gender or in culture – we grow as fit members of a society.

Truly, we are not meant to be alone, but to live in community. It is the social context in which our identity is defined and the human – the "image of God" in us – is fully realized and made most visible.

Aristotle had a dim grasp of this when he said that to be able to live outside society – the *polis* – one must be either a god or a beast. This is why those who live as atomized individuals in lonely societies long for community, to connect to something recognizably human, even if only remote and virtual.

---

13. See, for instance, Andrew Kirk, "Theology from a Feminist Perspective," in *Men, Women and God*, ed. Kathy Keay (Basingstoke: Marshall Pickering, 1987).

3

The Fallout of the Fall

"Cain knew his wife, and she conceived and bore Enoch; and he built a city . . ."

"And Adam knew his wife again, and she bore a son and called his name Seth . . . At that time men began to call upon the name of the Lord."

Genesis 4:17, 25–26

There is a strand of thinking that sees culture – metaphorically summed up in the "building of a city" – as originating from the fall. Sociologists tend to underscore the fact that it was Cain who first built a city, and it was from his descendants that the beginnings of civilization eventually emerged. They settled the land, domesticated cattle, and invented the first artifacts of human arts and crafts.[1]

This suspicion that advances in material culture are somehow propelled by the drive towards autonomy, away from dependence on God, is a biblical theme prominently shown in the case of the building of the Tower of Babel and what scholars call its incipient "Titanism."

In popular culture, we somehow associate the city and civilization with worldly decadence, and rustic pastoral settings with pristine innocence. This thinking dates back philosophically to the writings of people like Jean Jacques Rousseau and the idea of a "noble savage," and in the literature of the Romantic movement, which reacted to the grime and social inequalities of industrial life and imagined an idyllic state of nature. This was picked up by

---

1. See, for instance, Jacques Ellul's *The Meaning of the City,* trans. Dennis Pardee (Grand Rapids, MI: Eerdmans, 1970 / Carlisle: Paternoster, 1997).

the hippies and other back-to-nature movements that began in the 1960s and was spiritualized by New Agers.

On the other hand, side by side with the theme of the "city as sin" is a strand of biblical narratives showing the gradual growth of culture and population and the spread of peoples into nations as originally desired by God. As has been observed, the biblical account begins with a garden and ends with the city.[2]

In Genesis 10, there is the "Table of Nations" which evolved from the natural migrations of the descendants of Noah to all corners of the earth after the flood. This is a positive etymological explanation to the origin of nations. The counter-narrative to this is the hubris that provoked the direct intervention of God, which led to the confusion of tongues and the scattering of the people of Babel in Genesis 11.

Running through the biblical narrative is this tale of two cities – Babylon and Jerusalem; and two ways of ascending to heaven – the ziggurat and Mt Sinai. Parallel to this are the two genealogies – the one in chapter 4 from the *Yahwist* narrative, which tracks the growth of humanity through the line of Cain; and the one in chapter 5 from the *Priestly* tradition, which traces the beginning of a new line from Adam to Noah, and expressly describes the line of Seth as a replacement to the cut-off line of the dead Abel.

This great divide between the sons of Cain and the sons of Seth is usually seen as the equivalent of the divide between the "Seed of the Woman" and the "Seed of the Serpent." The line of Cain issues in a terrible song of power and vengeance by Lamech; the line of Seth issues in prayer, the beginning of the human – *Enosh* – crying out and calling on God once again.

In the following reflections we shall see that the divide is a little more complex, that it is not a neat separation between those who are sophisticated, autonomy-seeking "culture bearers" and those who live simpler, more innocent and pristine lives as "faith bearers."

Legends of the Fall

The Reformers, reacting to the more optimistic Thomistic sense of the good in human nature, elaborated on the total fallout of the fall in their doctrine of "total depravity." What this means is that there is no part in us which has

---

2. See Richard J. Mouw, *When the Kings Come Marching In* (Grand Rapids, MI: Eerdmans, 1983).

remained untouched or unmarred by sin. The mind, the emotions, and the capacity for taking charge of creation all conked out.

The following points spell out some of the consequences on our socio-cultural life.

1) An epistemological crisis

There are suggestions that eating the fruit of the "tree of the knowledge of good and evil" is an act of self-determination, asserting the right to make one's own judgment of what is good and evil.[3] The woman was caught between two conflicting authorities – God who said that "in the day that you eat of it you shall die" (Gen 2:17), and the serpent who insinuated that "you shall not die, for when you eat of it, you shall be like God."

The woman looked at the tree, and decided for herself that it was good for food, a delight to the eyes and to be desired to make one wise (Gen 3:6). Cornelius Van Til, commenting on this passage, saw in this the empiricist's arrogation of God's authority as final arbiter of what is moral. God's question, "Where are you?" (Gen 3:9) was an anguished cry over the fact that from then on, the man and woman were no longer in their proper place.

We installed ourselves and our own human reasoning at the center of the universe, and hence lost a central reference point by which we can find absolute meaning and value. Like the seven blind men and the elephant, we mistake the part for the whole elephant, absolutizing our own limited perception of what the world must be like.

Sigmund Freud, for instance, saw the power of sexuality and attributed all our cultural achievements to the sex drive. B. F. Skinner, seeing people as completely manipulable through a system of rewards and punishments, proposed that we go beyond notions of freedom and dignity, since all we are is a product of such conditioning. Karl Marx, gripped by the insight that economics has such force that a man will always bow before the hand that feeds him, saw the overturning of economic relations as the one-answer solution to all our social ills.

Aristotle and modern sociologists enthroned society as primary shaper and defining mirror of who we are, the one place where we can be disciplined,

---

3. For Von Rad, the lure was not so much the prospect of extending knowledge as the independence that enables one to decide what helps or hinders, of going beyond the limits set by God at creation. It was a form of titanism or hubris; "better off as an autocrat than obedient to God," quoting E. Osterloh, *Evangelical Theology*, 1937, 439.

by order and tradition, into something fairly decent. This, and the over-reliance on rationality, is behind the undue optimism that education, or learning technologies, can civilize our brutish instincts and socialize us into wanting the "common good."

Philosophers painted themselves into a corner, lapsing into solipsism and doubting even the existence of the self, having no way of threading together into coherence the discrete sense impressions passing through their consciousness.

"Claiming to be wise, we became fools," said the Apostle Paul. Substituting the truth about God, ourselves and the world for our own social constructs, our thinking became "futile" and we became like Plato's cave men – ruminating on the shadows thrown on the walls by the sunlight behind our backs.

Lost in a sea of relativist claims, we long "to see life whole and to see it steadily," as Matthew Arnold put it. For as the Psalmist teaches us, "by Thy light we see light." It is only by returning to the Light, to our true center, that we truly see and know.

It is this truth that dawned on the Oxford don C. S. Lewis upon conversion. "I believe in God in the same sense that I believe the sun has risen," he says, "not because I see it, but because by it I see everything else."

2)   The sexual and social divide

Some scholars interpret the primeval sin as having something to do with wanting to be like the eternal God, achieving a kind of quasi-immortality through offspring produced by sexual intercourse. The Hebrew for "knowledge" has sexual connotations, as in "Adam *knew* Eve." The eating of the fruit is a symbol of the loss of innocence, of the passage from childhood through puberty to adulthood.[4]

However one may interpret this mythic gesture, the narrative clearly sets forth as a result the alienation between man and woman. The bond of being "soulmates," of commonality that enabled communion, was broken. In its place was shame before each other, and blame-shifting. Guilt before God made them hide and cower in fear, conscious of their nakedness. In Asian cultures, this hiding before God is present as a concept in the idea of a cosmic hide-and-seek, and in social terms took the form of a deep sense of shame that manifests itself in highly elaborate rituals of face-saving.

---

4. Bandstra, *Reading the Old Testament*, 68.

It is not true that the world can be divided into "guilt cultures" and "shame cultures." All cultures have some primal sense of a cosmic breakdown, of a "wrath shed abroad in the universe" that needs appeasing.

In primal cultures people sense this when disaster strikes and the crops are destroyed, or a plague makes the entire community sick. They then slit the throat of a white cock in the light of a pale moon, or kill a pig or a cow or some such sacrifice to satisfy the requirements of retribution. In what we call the "West," or secularized cultures, the sense of trouble in the cosmos may take the form of a nameless dread, which finds no relief because there is no one home in the universe to make an answer or grant absolution. A crime is treated as a social maladjustment. They call on the therapist to allay anxieties and tranquilize mental discomposure.

A most devastating consequence for women is the fall from dominion, from equal status as co-regent of the earth to subjection in both the domestic and social order (Gen 3:16).

The woman will experience domination as wife and pain as mother. She will suffer for the very things she most desires – a relationship and progeny. Her sexual desire shall undo her independence, and her procreative powers shall be exercised only at the cost of so much pain. Note that her subjugation is not prescriptive but predictive, "he shall rule over you." God in his foreknowledge warns her of the sorrow that lies ahead. This is not the original "state of nature," but a consequence of the woman usurping the place of God over his creation.

There is a notion that this subjection is punishment for the woman taking undue leadership over the man, luring him into temptation. This interpretation has a long history, as can be seen in rabbinical and patristic readings of this text, which see the woman as seducer or at best deceived and ignorant.[5] The poet John Milton in *Paradise Lost* suggests that the man was not deceived, but ate anyway for love of the woman. He could not bear being separated from her.

Such interpretations are evidently extrapolations from present realities in many patriarchal cultures. It has been seriously advanced as an anthropological proposition that subordination of woman is creational since it can be observed as a universal phenomenon in all cultures. "The secondary

---

5. Even modern commentators take this position, seeing the woman's "desire" as a "violent craving, bordering on disease." He shall rule because she has usurped his headship: "By listening to his wife, when deceived by the serpent, Adam had repudiated his superiority to the rest of creation . . ." See Delitzsch, *Pentateuch*, 103.

status of women is one of the true universals, a pan-cultural fact . . . It exists within every type of social and economic arrangement, and in societies of every degree of complexity."[6]

The empirical basis for this claim is rather doubtful. It is certainly not true among our upland cultures, whether among the Aetas or the more sophisticated Cordillera peoples. Not to mention our pre-Hispanic culture, where the female *babaylan* – who was repository of literary and medical lore – was recognized as one of the four pillars of society, along with the *datu* (chief), the *bayani* (warrior), and the *panday* (metalworker or craftsman).[7]

What could be safely said is that under fallen circumstances, male-female relationships have indeed deteriorated. In ancient Near Eastern cultures, women were either worshiped as fertility gods or treated as chattel. In this and other Latin-influenced countries, women are even now put on a pedestal like the Madonna or treated as a whore.

The truer biblical picture is that Adam and Eve both failed in their proper exercise of leadership. The woman listened to the serpent, a creature whose craftiness she could have mastered. The man listened to his wife, abdicating the responsibility to keep both of them in place within the order of God's creation. While the woman was the more active partner, the man was nevertheless passively acquiescent to the inordinate grasping for knowledge beyond the limits set by God.

It was not long after this that the existential question, "where are you?" was followed by the social question, "where is your brother?"[8] The refusal to accept human limits – "you shall be as God" – soon issued in the refusal to accept human solidarity – "am I my brother's keeper?"

Atlas Shrugged, the title of Ayn Rand's novel, echoes in our time Cain's reply from the distant past. This hymn to unfettered individualism and capitalism, or the neo-liberal idea that the poor are best left to market forces, is traceable to that first refusal to be bothered with one's neighbor.

---

6. Sherry B. Ortney, "Is Female to Male as Nature Is to Culture?" in *Women, Culture and Society*, eds. Michelle Zimbalist Rosaldo and Louise Lamphere (Stanford, CA: Stanford University Press, 1974).

7. Fe Mangahas and Jenny Romero-Llaguno, *Centennial Crossings: Readings in Babaylan Feminism in the Philippines* (Quezon City: C and E Publishing, 2006).

8. Von Rad, *Genesis*, 106.

3) *Life narrows to economics*

The serpent was not altogether misleading: Adam and Eve did get to know good and evil. Before the fall, all they knew was good; evil was beyond their experience.[9] Unsatisfied with a merely intellectual knowledge of evil – "in the day that you eat of it you shall die" (Gen 2:17) – they wanted to know it experientially, to spread their wings, so to speak, and travel beyond the confines of the good world whose shadows they do not know.

But instead of expansion, of being able to run free to explore the height and depth and breadth of unknown territory, life got narrowed to grubbing for a living. "By the sweat of your face you shall eat bread" (Gen 3:19, ESV), God tells Adam. Because nature would no longer yield readily to his will – "thorns and thistles it shall bring forth to you" (Gen 3:18) – he will have to work hard just to be able to eat.

It is a fact that much of our waking life is now occupied by work: "All the toil of man is for his mouth," Ecclesiastes tells us (Eccl 6:7). Economics now dominates our lives; while most of us are not at all Marxists in theory, in practice we validate his thesis that economics is the substructure of human social life. Much of the choices we make are determined and shaped by what to most of us is the bottom line – economics.

Not only is there no time to smell the flowers; often, the rewards are not commensurate to the labor we have expended. The poor work at 3D jobs – dirty, dangerous and dirt-cheap – and even these are scarce. Our young people, desperate for work, get sucked into the global industry of business process outsourcing as nocturnal cyberslaves.

It is in work that we most clearly see the descent of Adam from masterful dominion to futility and alienation from the earth. He fell, not just from innocence to maleficence, but also from a sense of mastery to misery, from power to helpless degradation into mere cogs in the machine, replaceable by technology and easily made redundant.

Along with him, the earth groans, cursed because of us. And so nature strikes back with disasters, plagues, famines and other "acts of God" that on closer look are mostly man-made, byproducts of our bad stewardship of the earth.

---

9. Cf. Von Rad, *Genesis*. The Hebrew *yd* – to know – "never signifies purely intellectual knowing, but in a much wider sense an 'experiencing,' a 'becoming acquainted with,' even an 'ability' ... For the ancients the good was not just an idea: the good was what had a good effect, what was beneficial or salutary and detrimental or damaging" (Ibid., 89).

4)   *The anthill or the superman*

On the whole, the true nature of human sin is this overweening pride that makes us want to break out of the limits of our creatureliness.

"You shall be as God," said the serpent. It is true that there is a whole realm, like the mystery of death and evil, that lies beyond our grasp. And God knows the whole of it, and even experienced it as a human being in his Son. But unlike us, he can know it intimately without being overcome by it.

The first humans, wanting to know more, sought to experience good and evil, just like God. But then unlike God, we cannot know evil and not get contaminated and burnt by it.

The story of Lot is instructive. It is said that he pitched his tent and dwelt nearer and nearer to Sodom, attracted by that great and decadent city (Gen 13:12–13). He ended up running for his life when the city burned because of its wickedness, and had to dwell in a cave and, in drunkenness, incestuously sired offspring by his own daughters.

Evil, at first instance, never looks ugly; it is seductively full of glamour and sophisticated bonhomie, making us feel somehow deprived and confined when our lives are full of stark simplicity, having chosen to live with the disciplines of generosity and goodness in a world of scarcity. To this day, we continue to believe the lie of the serpent. Our gurus tell us that with the right meditation techniques or a shift in our social paradigms, we shall finally awaken to our true self – superman or the god within us.

With the downfall of the altar of God, says the Russian novelist Fyodor Dostoyevsky, humanity is left with either the anthill or the superman. With prophetic prescience, Dostoyevsky foresaw the social consequences of losing our sense of proportion once God is out of the way. We either deify the collective and sacrifice everything to an abstract good as defined by anonymous authorities, or elevate ourselves to the status of supermen – brilliant criminals like Raskolnikov to whom "everything is permitted," or, as Milton's satanic character Belial puts it, "free and to none accountable."

Those of us who have lived through authoritarian regimes ruled by despots or totalitarian states gripped by the iron claws of military junta know where this sort of thinking can lead us.

4

Culture and the Nations

Today you are driving me from the land, and I will be hidden from your presence; I will be a restless wanderer on the earth, and whoever finds me will kill me.

Genesis 4:14 (NIV)

There is some truth to the idea that culture – or the making of cities – is somehow propelled by the effort to make life bearable without God.

Cain, driven by fear and bound to the land as tiller of the soil, has been tragically alienated and uprooted from it. He has to fend for himself in ways available to him. Now living in a violent world, the city was a way of barricading his clan from the assault of avenging tribes and marauders. Yet running as a counter-theme to this story of crime and punishment is the story of how God's redemptive mercy can be found at the very places where we experience the depths of our descent to perdition.

We see this early in what theologians call the "proto-evangelium" – the first announcement of the gospel – the promise that the "seed of the woman" shall eventually crush the "seed of the serpent" (Gen 3:15). Here, the role of the woman is reversed, from gateway to sin to bearer of the seed that will overturn evil.

This redemptive thread runs through the efforts of primeval peoples to live in the tension between "the rainbow and the curse," between the promise of posterity and the inevitability of death, between the reality of sin and the strength of grace in human life. Interwoven as warp and woof of the fabric of our lives is the good and the bad, or, as the literati would put it, the sublime and the ridiculous.

We shall follow these two threads in the biblical account and explore what it means for our time.

Death's Tender Mercy

It is significant that after the fall, the woman acquires a new name, Eve. The intimate connection between man and woman now broken, the emphasis is no longer sameness –she is *ishshah* to his *ish* – but the procreative task of racial survival, of just keeping alive and mothering the living.

Previous to this, a glimmer of hope was held out to the woman as the sentence on the serpent was pronounced: "I will put enmity between you and the woman, and between your seed and her seed; he shall bruise your head, and you shall bruise his heel."[1] Not only is the serpent cursed above all wild animals, its once proud form is degraded into a slimy creature now crawling on its belly and eating dust. There shall be this constant antagonism between the woman's offspring and his, and in the end the serpent shall be crushed.

Delitzsch underscores the meaning of this massive grace:

> The fact that the victory over the serpent is promised to the posterity of the woman, not of the man, acquires this deeper significance, that as it was through the woman that the craft of the devil brought sin and death into the world, so it is also through the woman that the grace of God will give to the fallen human race the conqueror of sin, of death, and of the devil.[2]

Likewise, the banishment of Adam and Eve from paradise for fear that they might eat of the fruit of the tree of life is symbolic of God's continuing care for his creatures. There is the notion that Adam and Eve were driven out for fear that they would become truly godlike. This is seen as similar to the threatened Greek gods punishing Prometheus for stealing fire. On the contrary, this act of banishment was in fact a mercy: in their altered condition, to eat of the fruit of the tree of life, and live forever, would be eternal misery.

A legend goes that a Sibyl asked the gods to give her eternal life. The tricky Greek gods, being what they are, granted her wish for eternal life, but without giving her eternal youth. As a consequence, she just got older and older, bent and heavily wrinkled and weary of life. When children in the village would

---

1. Ibid.
2. Franz Delitzsch, *A New Commentary on Genesis*, Vol. 1 (Grand Rapids, MI: Eerdmans, 1951), 102.

taunt and ask the old woman, "What is it you want?" the wizened Sybil would reply, "I want to die."

It is a mercy that in our condition, we die and do not go on and on like a badly resuscitated Frankenstein. It is resurrection, not a disembodied immortality nor a robotic humanoid assembled by a madman, that God promises as an answer to death and decay and the brevity of life.

I got an appreciation of this at close range when a well-loved aunt celebrated her 100th birthday. Upon leaving, I casually remarked that I was looking forward to seeing her again at her 101st birthday party. She smirked in her rather comical and straightforward way and said, "No. I don't want another year. It is boring *na*." All her friends had died and she had been reduced to merely looking out her window at dusk, alone with her memories. As was her wish, she refused to eat and duly died a month or so before her 101st.

The Curse of Rootlessness

Exile, or this painful uprooting from the land that once served as one's original habitat, is increasingly a universal experience in a time when masses of people have become globally mobile.

Driven by the evils of poverty or political turmoil, or merely the thirst for adventure and the restless search for opportunity among postmodern "global vagabonds," many are now experiencing a massive rootlessness. Migrants are being pushed and pulled into the vortex of global centers that have become like kitchen sinks sucking the dregs of human economic and political misery.

While we may not be aware of it, this rupture of ties between land and people is what the "curse of Cain" is all about. Because the earth – *adama* – cries out with the blood of Abel, it denies Cain its blessing: "When you till the ground, it shall no longer yield to you its strength" (Gen 4:12). Instead of a settled farming life, this tiller of the soil was condemned to wander as a fugitive in the land of Nod, land of flight and banishment. This estrangement from his original vocation he could hardly bear, and the city, we surmise, was perhaps a contrived way of grounding himself into a settled existence.

There is a suggestion in the narrative that being driven from the land means extreme vulnerability: "Behold, thou hast driven me this day away from the ground; and from thy face I shall be hidden; and I shall be a fugitive and a wanderer on the earth, and whoever finds me will slay me" (Gen 4:14).

Being cut off from the land means being out in the shadows, at the edges of that protective circle of light cast by the watchful eye of God's presence.

"Banishment from the soil meant banishment to the desert places, the refuge of demons and outlaws."[3] Cain now feels himself to be a helpless prey to the violence of those exacting blood revenge.

"Not so!" was God's ringing declaration that he is not without protection. "If anyone slays Cain, vengeance shall be taken on him sevenfold" (Gen 4:15). This "mark of Cain" is perhaps a tribal tattoo that warns other clans of the ferocity of reprisal, hence serving as his protection from possible avengers.

Similarly, it is not necessarily a sign of God's negative judgment on culture that it was Cain and his descendants who built cities.[4] It may in fact be a sign of grace, that the creative and inventive gifts in-built into human nature did not cease to be operative in sinful men and women but instead were harnessed to make fallen life livable.

In the face of violence, scarcity and a hardscrabble life, Cain's line constructed cities, domesticated animals, fashioned tools that formed the beginnings of copper and iron industries, and found comfort and solace in the beginnings of the fine arts, crafting and playing musical instruments like the lyre and pipe (Gen 4:20–22).

Alongside this growth of human culture is of course also the exponential growth of sin, facilitated and made more lethal by the technologies invented. This is evident in the "Song of the Sword," Lamech's boasting that he has slain a man who merely wounded him. The "striking" and "bruising" was made by a fist; the "slaying" was by the thrust of a sharp sword. Lamech boasts of his increased capacity to inflict revenge: "If Cain is avenged sevenfold, truly Lamech seventy-seven fold" (Gen 4:24). Security is no longer in relying on divine protection, but in the possession of superior weaponry.

The idea that technology can be Faustian – that is, overly ambitious in breaking through the limits of human powers – has truth in it. This overreaching is prefigured by the account of a mysterious union between what appears to be angels – "sons of god" – and daughters of men, which gave rise to the Nephilim, the "mighty ones" or superheroes (Gen 6:1–4). This hybrid of a superior race seems to be part of an ungodly effort to maximize human powers: "God's spirit and life-giving power entered mankind far

---

3. Keil and Delitzsch, *Pentateuch*.

4. Delitzsch saw in Cain's building of the city "a desire to neutralize the curse of banishment, and create for his family a point of unity, as a compensation for the loss of unity in fellowship with God" (Keil and Delitzsch, *Pentateuch*, 117).

beyond the original design at creation."[5] Hence, God has set a maximum age beyond which unredeemed humanity cannot go.

Scholars note that the genealogies are "a witness to the great vitality of the first men in procreation." Alongside this, however, is the onward march of time and decay, which can be seen in the gradual diminishing of the human life span: 1,000 to 700 years from Adam to Noah, 600 to 200 from Noah to Abraham, 200 to 100 years by the time of the patriarchs.[6] Delitzsch considers this a "transitional period, during which death caused by sin slowly broke the powerful physical resistance of primitive human nature."

This inexorable degeneration is something that even our modern technologies cannot hope to reverse. It is mere illusion to think that with our life-support machines, we are actually prolonging life. The truth is we are really only prolonging the process of dying.

The Origin of Nations

The biblical narrative has two accounts of how life spread on earth. We have the *Priestly* account in Genesis 10, which is entirely devoted to the sons of Noah and tells of the natural migrations of people who are born, settle, create cultures and become nations. Then there is the *Yahwist* story in Genesis 11, where Yahweh intervenes directly in human dispersion.[7]

It was observed that the two accounts "seem strangely out of order. The Tower of Babel story presumes a unitary human population that disperses after God confused their language. But the Table of Nations precedes it and locates peoples in their places around the world."[8] But then it will be noticed that both accounts tell the same story of post-flood human growth, consistent with the command to "be fruitful and multiply." Also, in the *Yahwist* account, human nature did not change even after the cleansing effort of the Flood.

We shall have more to say about the Tower of Babel and the intentional allocation of habitations for the peoples of the earth. For the moment, it is sufficient to note that in Genesis 10, we see the origin of peoples, the locations of their settlements and their languages.

---

5. Von Rad, *Genesis*, 114.

6. Ibid.

7. Norman Habel, *The Birth, the Curse and the Greening of Earth: An Ecological Reading of Genesis 1–11* (Sheffield: Sheffield Phoenix Press, 2011), 116.

8. Bandstra, *Reading the Old Testament*, 81.

The descendants of Japheth spread to the coastlands, populating maritime and coastal areas. In spite of the so-called "Hamitic curse,"[9] the descendants of Ham originated great cities – Egypt, Babylon, Nineveh – mostly by the legendary warrior Nimrod, who built four cities and established the first kingdom. Shem's descendants lead us to the Semitic tribes in Arabia, where pre-Abrahamic Israel was not distinguished at all.[10] It was to emerge only later, from the line of Arpachshad.

Genesis 10, quite significantly, recognizes the primordial diversity of culture. Theologians of the Middle Ages tended to view sin as cause of diversity. Most scholars glossed over or ignored the alternative tradition in Genesis 10. It is possible that this is due to selective perception, partly aided by the simple difference in source. The *Priestly* tradition puts emphasis on divine blessing and not sin, as in its versions of creation, the Flood, and the covenant with Noah.

> Chapters 1–7 tell a story of creation to destruction, and chapters 8–11 tell a story of divine grace in spite of continued human willfulness. The startling conclusion of the Primeval Story is that in the face of the post-flood return of sin, humanity does not meet the same fate as before the flood, but instead God singles out Shem, blesses his line, and creates a nation through it.[11]

The twin poles of sin and grace are seen in the effort to arrest the deterioration of creation by human contrivance and the natural process of cultural evolution. On the one side is the prideful mono-cultural project of the Tower of Babel, where God directly intervenes to make languages and cultures diverse. On the other side is the natural flow of migration, where various nations emerged from the descendants of Noah and domains of earth became habitats for diverse cultures.

There is a line of interpretation that the intent of Genesis 10 has little to do with geography. Its purpose is,

> (a) to show that Divine Providence is reflected in the distribution of the nations over the face of Earth no less than in other acts of the world's creation and administration; (b) to determine the

---

9. For a time, this terrible idea that the descendants of Ham, as prefigured by Canaan especially, are cursed to be slaves, provided theological legitimation to apartheid in South Africa.

10. Von Rad, *Genesis*, 140ff.

11. Bandstra, *Reading the Old Testament*, 86.

relationship between the peoples of Israel and other peoples; (c) to teach the unity of post-diluvian humanity, which, like ante-diluvian humanity, is wholly descended from one pair of beings.[12]

There is certainly a strong strain of Divine Providence in the evolution of the sons of Noah into nations as they spread abroad on the earth. Theologically, this is affirmed in the Song of Moses: "When the Most High gave to the nations their inheritance, when he separated the sons of men, he fixed the bounds of the peoples according to the number of the sons of God" (Deut 32:8–9). This is echoed in Paul's speech to the Athenians: "And he made from one every nation of men to live on all the face of the earth, having determined allotted periods and the boundaries of their habitation . . ." (Acts 17:26).

What this tells us is that nations are not just accidents of history or geography. The divine hand is active and present in the separation of peoples, and the cultures they make out of their interaction with the environments allotted to them. This runs counter to the current narrative that nationality and ethnicity are merely incidental, pegs on which we hang ourselves in a globalizing world.

It needs emphasizing that this culture-making has much to do with geography. "While an initial reading may give the impression that the focus is entirely on family histories, a close reading reveals that geography and genealogy are both integral to the development of cultures. Earth and the domains of Earth play a key role in the context and plot of these legends."[13]

Cultures evolve out of the interplay of land, climate and people, creating a secondary environment of tools, artifacts, conceptual systems and patterns of behavior that are learned historically through the generations. Our sense of time, for instance, is shaped by the nature of our seasons. Those of us in the tropics experience time seamlessly, the wet and dry cycle changing gently and almost imperceptibly. This makes for a sense of time that is focused on the present, whereas those who have to prepare and cope with severe winters tend to be futuristic, always anticipatory and anxiously wanting to plan ahead.

That God had a hand in the unique culture that emerges out of the human interaction with land and climate means that we take seriously the fact of our rootedness. "We are meant to get rooted in one place, embedded in the very

---

12. Umberto Cassuto, *A Commentary on the Book of Genesis, Part 2* (Jerusalem: Magnes Press, 1964), 175.

13. Habel, *Birth, the Curse and the Greening of Earth*, 117.

stone and rock formations of deserts and mountains or in the wild jungles of rain forests or in the ebb and flow of sand and sea."[14]

That God decreed our "times and seasons and the boundaries of our habitations" also means that all peoples would have developed "high cultures" if all had evolved without the tragic disruptions and depredations of conquering empires:

> Some perhaps would have remained Spartan in their material culture, like Israel in the desert settlements of Palestine, as compared to the highly wrought and structured civilizations of Egypt and Mesopotamia that grew round the Nile and the Tigris-Euphrates, or even China and the Indian subcontinent that flourished along the Ganges and the Yangtze rivers. But all would have preserved their unique insights and tools for life that they can bring to the table of nations, as promised in that final vision of the kings of the earth bringing the glory and riches of their nations into the New Jerusalem.[15]

On the whole, it would seem that even after the fall, God is able to weave a redemptive story out of the human longing for the solace and security afforded by the city. The city is not *a priori* negative, and progress in civilization is a positive part of the human story.[16]

Whether evolutionary or catastrophic, the development of culture is not to be seen as apposite to the Greek legend of Prometheus stealing fire. Along this line, some have thought that "The real revenge for Prometheus' act . . . is a promethean culture and civilization which, by its victories over the 'secrets' of our world, leads men gradually to despise and forget Zeus." In contrast, in the OT,

> No robbery is needed, no culture hero to rise in revolt against the gods and snatch from them the fire that makes civilization possible. It is a function of the blessing God bestows on his creatures to enable the creatures themselves to make the basic discoveries. Civilization and its effects then have a positive

---

14. Maggay, *Rise Up and Walk*, 215.

15. Ibid., 216.

16. Claus Westermann, *Genesis 1–11: A Commentary*, trans. John J. Scullion, first published 1974 (Minneapolis, MN: Augsburg Publishing House, 1984), 328. cf. Deut 6:10, "great and goodly cities, which you did not build."

emphasis in Israel from the very beginning; it is founded in God's will for his creatures.[17]

While the city can be a sign of self-reliance, or a "concealed Titanism," it is also a sign of our restored mastery over creation, a celebration of human achievement and joy in inventiveness.[18]

We are shown early signs of this positive theme in the four rivers flowing out of Eden, which functions as a mythic symbol of some organic connection and continuity between the blessings of paradise and the civilization that grew out of the Fertile Crescent. Likewise, in the birth of Noah, whose name means "comfort," his father Lamech saw the possibility of relief from the curse: "Out of the ground which the Lord has cursed this one shall bring us relief from our work and from the toil of our hands" (Gen 5:28–29).

In the Table of Nations, which stands between the flood and the beginning of redemptive history, we see the flourishing of culture at the close of the primeval age. Along with the Tower of Babel story, it sets the stage for the dawning of a new age in God's redemptive activity. Unlike legendary Near Eastern stories of the origin of places and cities, it is not "a mythical, prehistorical world of gods and monsters, but the sober, classifiable world of nations, territories, cities, kingdoms and languages – a thoroughly recognizable, political, human world."[19]

---

17. Westermann, commenting on J. P. Audet's notion that "the significance of religion has continually and irreversibly receded in the course of the millennia of human history, while the development of civilization by stealing the fire has become determinative for humankind in an ever-increasing degree" (Westermann, *Genesis 1–11*, 343).

18. Von Rad, *Genesis*, 144.

19. Christopher J. H. Wright, *Walking in the Ways of the Lord: The Ethical Authority of the OT* (Downers Grove, IL: InterVarsity, 1995), 218.

5

The Tower of Babel

*Now the whole earth had one language and few words . . . And
they said to one another, "Come, let us make bricks, and burn them
thoroughly." And they had brick for stone, and bitumen for mortar.
Then they said, "Come, let us build ourselves a city, and a tower with
its top in the heavens, and let us make a name for ourselves, lest we be
scattered abroad upon the face of the whole earth." . . . And the Lord
said, "Behold, they are one people, and they have all one language;
and this is only the beginning of what they will do; and nothing that
they propose to do will now be impossible for them."*

Genesis 11:1–6

Now that we are face to face as nations and cultures, we like to think
that the world has become a "global village" as Marshall McLuhan
had predicted. Intercultural studies show, however, that proximity does
not necessarily lead to understanding other cultures. It may in fact deepen
racial stereotypes.

The Japanese novelist Shūsaku Endō had long ago expressed pessimism
that there can be real understanding across cultures. We may, he said, go
through the motions of communicating. But in the end, between the East and
the West, there is really only silence.[1]

In the mid-1990s, the Social Development Summit at Copenhagen,
Denmark, saw the increasing crisis of multi-cultural societies and the need

---

1. See Shūsaku Endō's famous book, *Silence* (New York: Taplinger, 1979, first published
in 1966), the story of a Jesuit priest in the 17th century in the throes of doubt, longing to
break through the "silence" of God and between cultures as he sees Japanese Christians being
martyred for their faith.

for "social integration." Living in racially mixed and polyglot societies has brought to the surface the problem of how to treat the strange neighbor next door who does not speak the local language and does not even try to assimilate.

Countries that once dreamed of multiculturalism are finding that this kind of society is not easy to put together. The underclasses, feeling themselves crowded out of jobs and space, resent the migrants as competitors for resources and opportunities. Those with memories of an older, simpler time when people lived in communities where everyone else had the same color of skin, or shared a common religious tradition, feel threatened by the loss of their cultural heritage.

In reaction, governments seek to impose a semblance of unity by requiring migrants to learn the language and conform to the rules of the host culture. This tendency to enforce unity by uniformity is not new. In the age of empires, rulers like the Caesars sought to establish hegemony across vast territories by inventing quasi-religious cults that served as glue for the various ethnicities assembled under the empire.

Scripture opens at least two windows through which "social integration" can be glimpsed and analyzed. One window is the Tower of Babel project, where we see masses of people speaking one language and able to forge a kind of *unity by uniformity*. The other window is Pentecost, where by supernatural means people of various tongues hear the same message in their own language, a startling *unity through diversity*.

In the Tower of Babel we see a purely human project and the power of cultural uniformity. In Pentecost we see divine power at work through cultural diversity. This chapter will first explore what the Tower of Babel means for our time.

The Meaning of the City

This story has been viewed by scholars as "the climax of primeval history, whose meaning and scope are universal."[2] A "masterpiece of narrative art," its meanings are "mythic," that is, not in the sense of "untrue," but in the literary sense of having dense resonances in various times and among various peoples.

---

2. Bernhard Anderson, *From Creation to New Creation* (Minneapolis, MN: Fortress Press, 1994), 167–168.

It was, said the story, a time of migration: masses of people moved "from the east," or from the north, which was roughly the site of Mount Ararat in Armenia, going southwest. They found Shinar, or Babylon, which scholars say was the whole of Mesopotamia, and was built on a vast plain.[3] There they settled, and moved from the "distant darkness of primeval time into the clear light where history begins."[4] Von Rad states:

> This beginning betrays an acute historical observation; nationalities tend to emerge from great migrations. Large bands for some unknown reason find themselves on the move; suddenly they step out of the obscurity of their previous unhistorical existence into the light of history and climb to cultural power.[5]

Twice we hear the people speaking to one another about two significant moments: the discovery of a new technology, and the building of the city and a "tower with its top in the heavens" (Gen 11:3–4). This ability to consult and create consensus enables them to invent bricks out of unpromising material like clay and straw. By burning bricks thoroughly instead of sun-dried, they had a substitute for the hardness of stone, which was used for large buildings but could not be had in the land of Shinar. These descendants of Vulcan or Tubal-Cain also used asphalt or bitumen in place of mortar. These new technologies emboldened the people to embark on the ambitious project of building a city and a tower.

The building of the city has been interpreted as a "sign of self-reliance," and along with the tower, a "will to fame" and a "demonstration of greatness in the work of their hands . . . an overstepping of their limits."[6] It is an "attempt to grasp greatness, rather than waiting for God's blessing."[7] A more modern take on the tower is that it is a way of "conquering space, a rejection of Mother Earth, seeking their place in the skies."[8]

---

3. John Gill, *Genesis*, Newport Bible Commentary (Springfield, MO: Particular Baptist Press, 2010). First published as *Volume One, An Exposition of the Old Testament* (London: Aaron Ward, 1763–1766).

4. Westermann sees this migration as primeval peoples transitioning from a nomadic to a sedentary life. Their itinerary has three stages: departure, discovery, and settlement (Westermann, *Genesis 1–11*, 544).

5. Von Rad, *Genesis*, 148.

6. Ibid., 149; Westermann, *Genesis 1–11*, 554.

7. Bandstra, *Reading the Old Testament*, 83.

8. Habel, *Birth, the Curse and the Greening of Earth*, 124.

The building of the city, presumably, was to secure their being together as "one people" (Gen 11:6). Unlike Cain's previous effort to build a city, which was primarily for shelter and to secure his safety, this city was for walling themselves in for social cohesion, "lest we be scattered abroad upon the face of the whole earth" (Gen 11:4). The city was a defense, not just against the dangers of an existence where life can be "nasty, brutish and short," but against social disintegration.

This fear of scattering is said to be in direct disobedience to the command to "fill the earth," to spread themselves and make something out of the peculiar geographies that God desires the nations to inhabit and cultivate. It is a human instinct to cluster, to herd ourselves together when faced with threats – real or imaginary – especially in relation to the strange or the unknown. The building of the city is an effort to consolidate and protect, by their own devising, the borders that define them as "one people." It is an act of centralization, a sign of an inward drift towards reliance on merely sociological forces in maintaining unity.[9]

The tower, on the other hand, was to "make a name for ourselves." Scholars say that the tower could be a reference to the *ziggurat*, a staged tower common in ancient Babylon. The word is from the Akkadian *ziggratu* – "mountain peak" – mountains considered holy places where the gods dwelt, as with Zeus in Mt Olympus, Baal in Mt Saphon, or Yahweh in Mt Sinai. There were no mountains on the Mesopotamian plain, and so they had to construct artificial ones, like the ziggurats.[10]

Some scholars have suggested that the plan to build the tower had a religious, and even astrological, significance. The tower that reaches up to heaven – literally a phrase that means "whose top the heavens" – was said to have on it drawings that depicted signs of the Zodiac. The Akkadian name for Babylon – *bab-ilu* – literally means "gate of the gods." The Babylonians believed that their capital city, through their ziggurat, gave them access to the heavens.[11] In the same vein is the idea that the tower must have been in the spirit of "aspiring to invade God's realm."[12]

---

9. Compare Delitzsch: "The fact that they were afraid of dispersion is a proof that the inward spiritual bond of unity and fellowship, not only 'the oneness of their God and their worship,' but also the unity of brotherly love, was already broken by sin" (Delitzsch, *Pentateuch*, 173).

10. Bandstra, *Reading the Old Testament*, 84.

11. Ibid.

12. Habel, *Birth, the Curse and the Greening of Earth*, 125.

Very likely, the tower derived its motive force not primarily for the religious reason of reaching up to the heavens, but simply, as stated, to "make a name for ourselves." The real motive, says Delitzsch, was "their desire for renown, and the object was to establish a noted central point, which might serve to maintain their unity."[13]

Babylon in the second millennium BC was center of power in the known world. It was legendary for its cultural achievements, like the ziggurats, which were admired as a marvel of glazed colored tiles and could reach over 297 feet high.[14] The ancient Babylonians boasted of the height of their temples.[15]

The Hebrew word "shem" means "name." Previously, names were given by superiors to inferiors, like God giving names to Shem and Abraham.[16] This time, we see people trying to make a name for themselves, a desire to build their own reputation by their own engineering.[17] It is a movement towards autonomy, driven by the desire to push human possibilities to maximum greatness without waiting for God's direction and initiative.

On the whole, the city in this passage is a defensive human effort to build its own ramparts against dispersion and the consequent erosion of social cohesion. The tower is symbolic of the drive for self-definition and autonomy, of projects that try to overreach in the name of pride and vainglory. It is here where we see warrant for the French sociologist Jacques Ellul's sensing that the city – and much of human culture – may have originated in the drive to lessen vulnerability and optimize achievement in a world where God has ceased to be relevant in quieting the fears and fueling the aspirations of people.

A Landlocked Homogeneity

Facilitating the Tower of Babel project was the fact that they all had "one language and few words," a cultural uniformity that made consensus-building and a common aspiration possible. The Lord himself, seeing what they managed to build, exclaimed in amazement: "Behold, they are one people,

---

13. Delitzsch, *Pentateuch*, 173.

14. Von Rad, *Genesis*, 151.

15. Kevan, "Genesis," 87.

16. Martin Kessler and Karel Deurloo, *A Commentary on Genesis: The Book of Beginnings* (Mahwah, NJ: Paulist Press International, 2004) 92; and Laurence A. Turner, *Genesis, Readings: A New Biblical Commentary* (Sheffield: Sheffield Academic Press, 2009), 54.

17. Bandstra, *Reading the Old Testament*, 87.

and they have all one language; and this is only the beginning of what they will do . . ." (Gen 11:6).

Divine prescience foresaw the potential power of this kind of homogeneity: "Nothing that they propose to do will now be impossible for them" (Gen 11:6). The newer NIV version puts it this way: "If as one people speaking the same language they have begun to do this, then nothing they plan to do will be impossible for them."

God himself affirms that "speaking one language" makes a people, and binds them together in such a way that they gather force and are able to do things beyond their numbers. Linguistic unity is instrumental to group solidarity and the power of synergy.

So God "comes down," a counterpoint to the act of humans "going up," and strikes at the root of their power: "Come, let us go down, and there confuse their language, that they may not understand one another's speech" (Gen 11:7).

Was God threatened by this show of what a united people can do?

The question is raised by those who see in the story a parallel to the legend of Prometheus stealing fire from the gods and getting punished for it. The answer is perhaps, yes, if Yahweh is anything like the Greek gods. But he is not, and so we need to find some other explanation for the "babel of tongues" that he caused.

The fact that God "descends" to see the city and the tower that they had built cautions us against seeing the people's achievement as a threat. "Yahweh must draw near, not because he is nearsighted, but because he dwells at such tremendous height and their work is so tiny. God's movement must therefore be understood as a remarkable satire on man's doing."[18] Consistent with this is the sensing of some scholars that there is a touch of irony in the Lord's remark that "nothing they propose (*zamam*) will now be impossible *(batsar)*," a mimetic echo of Job's realization of God's sovereign power: "I know that no purpose *(mezimma)* of yours will be thwarted *(batsar)*."[19]

Irony or not, Von Rad tells us that the oldest version of this narrative represented the building of the tower as a threat to the gods, but the Yahwist source removed this feature.[20] That the story is an "etiological saga" of how

---

18. Von Rad, *Genesis*, quoting Procksch, 149.

19. Habel, quoting Job 42:2, *Birth, the Curse and the Greening of Earth*, 125.

20. Von Rad, *Genesis*, 151.

languages came about brings us back to why God intervened directly to make this happen. The nature of language as a window to culture gives us a clue.

That they had "one language," or literally "one lip," tells us that we are dealing here with a society whose linguistic uniformity lends them capacity to be on the same page and organize projects of the magnitude of the Tower of Babel. That they had "few words," or a limited vocabulary, suggests a self-enclosed society walled in by its own technology, impoverished in words for lack of contact with a wider world.

Linguists have brought to our attention the fact that language is not just an instrument for voicing ideas, but shaping those very ideas.[21] We have no eyes and ears for things we have no words for.[22] Filipinos do not have an indigenous word for "privacy," for instance, being a culture that does not wall in a space where others cannot go. Intercultural studies tell us that Eskimos have at least seventeen different words for snow; they can discern the fine gradations of that white flaky thing which to us in the tropics is simply just that – snow. Filipinos, on the other hand, have an elaborate language for describing inner states of feeling, or those highly calibrated emotions going on within the *loob* or "inside" – like *sama ng loob, mababang loob, lakas ng loob, utang na loob* and so on. The sheer richness of concepts and words round the *loob* gives us a clue that we are dealing with a people with a highly-developed interiority, versed in naming the minutely delicate feelings going on inside. The Arabs likewise have a host of words related to camels and horses.

What all this means is that the people of Shinar, for all their technological achievements, could be fairly surmised to be somewhat parochial and delimited in their imagination of what the vast world can be like. As has been observed, "the limits of our language are the limits of our world."[23]

Think of the immense riches we all would have missed if the world were monocultural and had only one language. This is not the design of God for the world and the people in it. As we have seen earlier, we are meant to grow and fill the vast and empty earth with the work of our hands. We are to make the earth yield its richness, its variety of design and the ways of life that are possible given its lush and immense copiousness.

---

21. The Edward Sapir-Benjamin Whorf hypothesis.

22. Cf. William James' remark: "We have no eyes but for those aspects of things which have been labeled for us."

23. A quote from Suzanne Langer.

God desires nations to rise and inhabit the whole earth and develop a variety of cultures out of their geographies. We are not to get landlocked into the narrow confines of homogeneity.

A Babel of Tongues

The confusion that ensued upon God's intervention led to the scattering of the people and put a stop to the building of the city.

This confounding of the language need not be seen as a sudden event that is miraculous. "The confounding of the language may have been by a providential direction and hastening of the natural tendencies of men to form dialects, on the basis of which they would separate into various groups with differing sympathies and interests."[24]

There is a note of derision in calling the place "Babel," which has the same root and sound as the Hebrew *balal*, which means "confusion" or a mishmash of words popularly invented. Scholars note that Babel is also the way the Hebrew language writes Babylon.[25] From being the "gate of the gods," Babel became a testament to the eventual failure of projects born out of a monumental hubris.

This brings us to the second reason why God confused their language, besides forcing them, in a backhanded way, to go and fill the earth.

Fallen people, left to their own devices, are likely to direct their energies on projects that have no known functional significance apart from feeding the fires of vanity. What, for instance, is the point of building a tower that touches the sky? Or, for that matter, skyscrapers that seek the reputation of being the "tallest building in the world?" At bottom, it is a rather useless claim to fame whose utility is purely for "making a name for ourselves."

Imagine what it would be like if we had too many hare-brained schemes on such a scale. This country has had a taste of it during Ferdinand Marcos' authoritarian regime. Massive resources were funneled towards Imelda Marcos' "edifice complex," a tendency among those in power to immortalize themselves in shrines of wood and stone. It runs through all of history, from the primeval people of Babylon to Egypt's Pharaohs, to the great Solomon then on to Herod and our own modern Nimrods.

---

24. Kevan, "Genesis," 87.

25. Bandstra, *Reading the Old Testament*, 83.

But there is more to this failed project apart from the preventive and punitive intervention of a God who thwarts our prideful ambitions and our capacity for organized opposition. There is grave danger to it. Delitzsch puts it this way: "By the firm establishment of an ungodly unity, the wickedness and audacity of men would have led to fearful enterprises."[26] By confusing and scattering them, God prevented the "sin of humans from reaching such global and corporate dimensions as to render life on earth intolerable."[27]

A monocultural society has its strong points. We communicate with each other more efficiently, and there is a solidarity unmatched by societies wracked by linguistic and ethnic differences. Many account our fractiousness as a people, for instance, to the archipelagic nature of the country's terrain. We are all little islands speaking about 120–175 languages, depending on how they are classified. Other linguistic scholars say, however, that there is more unity than diversity among our indigenous languages; about 60 percent of our languages from north to south have strong similarities.[28]

At any rate, the story of the confusion of languages and the ensuing scattering gives us insight on why linguistically diverse societies tend to have difficulties becoming cohesive nations. And the Tower of Babel is a magnificent monument to what people are capable of doing when the society is homogeneous, or when an organization speaks the same language.

Today, we see the same movement towards centralization and homogenization, but also towards social disintegration and cultural fragmentation. There is, on the one hand, a Shinar-like movement towards clustering in global centers. Driven by technology and the market, there is a coming together of economic and social forces, a concentration of wealth and cultural influence. On the other hand, there is also a Babel-like scattering into ancient ethnic units as nation-states collapse. Tribes and peoples overrun by colonial and ideological empires in past centuries are reclaiming the old boundaries, the spaces originally allotted to them for their habitation.

The centrifugal movement forces conformity to a homogenizing global order that rides roughshod over the integrity of local cultures. The centripetal forces break down societies into ethnic minorities asserting self-

---

26. Delitzsch, *Pentateuch*, 173–174.

27. Wright, *Walking in the Ways of the Lord*, 28.

28. Dr Prospero Covar, in a remark to the author in an anthropological linguistics class, 1992.

determination, and reduces nations into fragile states in an almost permanent state of conflict and anomie.

This story warns us that "scattering" or diaspora movements are a sign of God's judgment on a wicked nation, as articulated by prophets like Jeremiah and Ezekiel.[29] Disobedience within nations eventually leads to chaos and a forced diaspora: "Whereas chapter 1 moved from chaos (*tohu wabohu*, 1:2) to order and rest, (*sabat*, 2:1–3), Babel reverses the move, beginning with order ('the whole earth had one language and the same words') and ending with chaos ('therefore it was called Babel, because there the Lord confused the language of the whole earth,' 11:9)."[30]

Shinar is a safe but narrow land. It is without the stress and discomfort of having to live next door to peoples of strange tongues and customs. In a time of so much land, its people have chosen to wall themselves in, kept within the limited vocabulary of a single language and boxed by the strait and demarcated confines of a city.

It is a symbol of self-enclosed cultures that pretend to be global when they are actually monocultural. The only difference of this kind of homogenized societies from the small city-states of ancient times or the old provincial town is that they happen to be in possession of technologies that allow them to project themselves and make over the rest of the world according to their own image.

In truth, the so-called "global village" is mostly the dominant cultures' perception of the world writ large on the canvas of today's social landscape via global media. What do we know about the latest terrorist bombings or flash points of conflict in the world apart from the images CNN or the BBC feeds us?

Mass travel in our time is making it possible for many cultures to at least take a good look at each other. Unfortunately, proximity is not a guarantee that we will understand each other, even in migrant-friendly global cities. Often, the sight of other races within sniffing distance tends to harden rather than break down stereotypes. That is why we see angry ethnic riots, neo-Nazi political parties, and young British Muslims aggrieved by growing up under a cloud of prejudice signing up for jihad as idealized by extremists.

---

29. Cf. Israel gathered in Ezekiel 11:16ff, Kessler and Deurloo, *Commentary on Genesis*, 92.

30. Turner, *Genesis*, 53.

There is a hidden mercy, however, in this story of the origin of linguistic diversity. Some from the "underside of history" would read this, for instance, as a resistance narrative among indigenous peoples.

> Christian Aboriginal people point to the story of the Tower of Babel as further biblical support for our belief that the culture and land of Australia are God-given. The story in Genesis ends with people being given different languages and moving off in different directions as a result of God's intervention. Language is a bearer of all culture; the Aboriginal languages are no less bearers of culture than the languages of other lands.[31]

Genesis 11 marks the end of primeval history and ushers in a new thread in Scripture's grand narrative: redemptive history.

With the Tower as symbol of human pride and rebellion, it could be asked: "Is God's relationship to the nations now finally broken; is God's gracious forbearance now exhausted; has God rejected the nations in wrath forever?" Von Rad, answering his own question, points to the

> strangely new thing that now follows the comfortless story about the building of the tower: the election and blessing of Abraham. ... From the multitude of nations God chooses a man, looses him from tribal ties, and makes him the beginner of a new nation and the recipient of great promises of salvation. What is promised to Abraham reaches far beyond Israel; indeed, it has universal meaning for all generations on earth.[32]

Scholars have been much exercised by having to account for the precise relationship between the first eleven chapters of Genesis and the beginnings of "sacred history." It would seem that the larger human canvas of primeval history actually prepares us for the staging of God's final act of redeeming humankind.

Throughout the narrative, there is this thread of sovereign grace running through epochal movements of human sin: Adam and Eve are clothed, Cain gets protected, the earth's stability is guaranteed by the rainbow after the flood, the longevity of "sons of god" is curtailed, and the autonomous effort

---

31. Quoting Rainbow Spirit Elders, leaders of aborigenes from Queensland, Australia, Habel, *Birth, the Curse and the Greening of Earth*, 123.

32. Von Rad, *Genesis*, 153–154.

at social integration, security and cultural achievement results in a divine-induced diaspora that births diverse nations.

"Babylon" as symbol of the prideful city, of the powerful and sinful drive to achieve collective security and fame apart from God, eventually gets transmuted into Jerusalem as *civitas dei,* two poles of human culture that, on the one hand, can be an organized center of hubris, and on the other, a "city on a hill," a beacon of light and hope for the nations.

Part II

The "Global Village": Living in a Multicultural World

6

Sojourners Together

Do not oppress an alien; you yourselves know how it feels to be aliens, because you were aliens in Egypt . . .

The alien living with you must be treated as one of your native-born. Love him as yourself, for you were aliens in Egypt. I am the Lord your God.

Exodus 23:9, Leviticus 19:34 (NIV 1984)

Transnational labor migration is not a new thing. In the age of empires and colonialism people have been transported as slaves or indentured labor. What is new perhaps is the overwhelming number of mass migrations, mostly economic and political refugees from impoverished countries and rogue states.

Both history and the Bible tell us that large masses of people residing within a nation not their own make them especially vulnerable to hostility and abuse from the host culture. This was the story of Israel in Egypt, and of other subject peoples under alien empires.

Today's globalization has surfaced the increasing conflict between human rights and citizenship rights. Before this, both human and citizenship rights were tied together within the nation-state. Now migrant populations are seen as threats to the native-born's citizenship rights. We see this especially in multiracial global centers that have imported migrant workers. Their underclasses perceive migrants as threats to their jobs, culture and living space.

How are we to look at the alien in our midst? How do we treat those who have come to dwell among us? The following explores some perspectives on the theme of the sojourner in Scripture.

Not Exactly Alien

In the Old Testament, the words *zar* (foreigner) and *nokri* (stranger) are used to denote those who come from a far-off land and are temporarily in contact with Israel as traders, travelers or soldiers. Both words generally have a negative connotation, either as an enemy or a threat to the religion and established order of Israel. They are barred from participating in the religious practices of Israel, and excluded from ascending to the throne or receiving the privilege of interest-free loans granted to impoverished Israelites.[1]

In contrast, there are at least two types of foreigner that are given access to the religious rites and economic protection under the Mosaic law. The *toshab* is a resident alien who is economically dependent, like a hired servant, and usually paired with *ger* (sojourner) in its narrowest sense a term for a person attached to a household, but not an actual member of the family, most likely an employee (1 Kgs 17:20; Job 19:15). The *ger* is a technical term used for a particular social status, carefully distinguished from and standing between the "native" and the "foreigner."[2]

The *ger* is for the most part treated as an ordinary Israelite, with economic rights such as rest on the Sabbath, a share in the triennial tithe, the produce of the land during the Sabbatical year, and gleaning rights. Politically, the *ger* has a right to fair trial, and provided he has completely identified with the covenant community, including circumcision, has access to religious observances like the Day of Atonement, the Passover, the Feast of Unleavened Bread, sacrificial and purification rites.[3]

The general impression regarding the treatment of foreigners in OT legislation is that there is both an affirmation of their rights as human persons, but also their exclusion from Israel's covenant rights and obligations if they have remained as outsiders to the faith of Israel.

The *zar* and *nokri* seem to be those aliens who have remained attached to their old homelands and have refused association with the culture and religion

---

1. For a helpful word study, see Narry Santos' "Tagapamagitan: A Cultural Bridge for Loving the Sojourner," in *The Gospel in Culture: Contextualization Issues through Asian Eyes,* ed. Melba Padilla Maggay (Mandaluyong, Metro Manila: OMFLiterature, 2013), 451–491. Also D. I. Block, "Sojourner, Alien, Stranger," in *The International Standard Bible Enclopedia,* vol. 4, ed. Geoffrey W. Bromiley (Grand Rapids, MI: Eerdmans, 1982).

2. R. J. D. Knauth, "Alien, Foreign Resident," in *Dictionary of the OT Pentateuch,* eds. T. Desmond Alexander and David W. Baker (Downers Grove, IL: InterVarsity, 2003), 26–33 (27).

3. See such economic rights as the triennial tithe, Deut 14:28–29; prompt wages, Deut 24:14–15; Sabbath rest Exod 20:10, 23:12; Deut 5:14, in Santos, "Tagapamagitan," 454–455.

of Israel. The *toshab* and the *ger* were those who seem to have voluntarily and completely identified with the spiritual values of Israel, including worship of their God.

Israel's memory of slavery in Egypt had deeply shaped its social legislation regarding the foreigner. Because they were once aliens as well, economic refugees who in time were reduced to slavery, they were told not to oppress the sojourner. Instead, they were to "love" them (Exod 22:21; 23:9; Deut 10:18–19).

In fact, the sojourner was to be treated as "a native among you," enjoying the same right to justice and equity as a native-born of Israel (Lev 19:34). There should be no disparity in her access to the civil rights guaranteed by the law: "You shall have one law for the sojourner and for the native; for I am the Lord your God" (Lev 24:22).

Scripture is well aware of the vulnerability of sojourners in a foreign land. It ranks the alien with the poor, the fatherless and the widow in defenselessness, as well as the need for special provision (Lev 24:19–22). Thus, the law entitles him to economic rights, and God himself stands in his defense and will judge those who oppress him (Exod 23:12; Lev 19:10; 23:22; Ps 94:6; Jer 7:6; 22:3; Ezek 22:7, 29). Clearly, the current chasm between human rights and citizenship rights cannot be countenanced from Scripture.

This divide can be traced historically from the "political rights" tradition of western liberalism. The idea that societies come together because of a "social contract," with rights and obligations spelled out between the rulers and the ruled, has given rise to a body of civic knowledge that puts emphasis on the rights and responsibilities of people belonging to a nation-state. In the modern world, this has liberated subject peoples from the chains of sacralized monarchies.

With the drift towards secular populism, however, this has also cut off the language of "rights" from its more fundamental roots: the inviolable nature of human beings, whether as individuals or as a collective. The "human rights" tradition originally derived inspiration from the Judeo-Christian idea that people are made in the image of God. This "image" gives them absolute value.[4] This idea has been obscured and eroded by modern secularism, such that in spite of the overdeveloped language for "rights" in western secular

---

4. Some see this as the basis for capital punishment: "Whoever sheds the blood of man, by man shall his blood be shed; for God made man in his own image" (Gen 9:6).

societies, ethnic minorities have been subjected to discrimination and increasing hostility.

In the age of globalization, market forces have driven migrant labor to emergent economies whose cultures and institutions lack norms that could serve as basis for human rights. Within the Asia region and the Arab world, abuse of migrant workers and other non-citizens has been particularly acute. This has been attributed to such factors as authoritarianism in these regions, the lack of a deep enough philosophical basis for human rights in these cultures, and the priority put on economic development over and against civil and political rights.

There is need to revisit the idea of "universal human rights" as originally articulated in Scripture if we are to protect our people who cross borders to seek opportunities in the fast-moving exchange of goods and services going on globally.

Migrant Rights, Pluralism and Cultural Integrity

In the interface of cultures, the migrant has to live the tension between keeping her ethnic identity and adjusting to the host culture. Likewise, the host country is faced with the demands of hospitality and the call of shared humanity alongside the need to preserve its own cultural integrity.

This tension is addressed in Scripture by a number of laws detailing correct behavior in Israelite society. Even as foreigners, those who live within the borders of Israel were to subject themselves to the discipline of its moral and spiritual laws. Aliens were to refrain from immorality, idolatry and blasphemy (Lev 18:6; 20:2; 24:16). They were to respect Israel's laws on ritual purity. They were to respect the nation's holy days, like not eating leaven on the Feast of Unleavened Bread, and not working on the Sabbath and on the Day of Atonement (Exod 12:19; 20:10; Lev 16:29). However, they could eat unclean meat, and were not compelled to keep the Passover (Deut 14:21; Exod 12:48).

It would seem that there was, on the one hand, a concern to preserve Israel's sense of its unique identity as the people of God. On the other hand, there was sufficient tolerance for the foreigner's cultural and religious autonomy. The freedom from Jewish dietary rules was a concession to the outsider's culture. The stricture to do as Israel does when it comes to its moral and spiritual life was a way of guarding the purity of the nation.

Surrounded by heathen neighbors, Israel had a profound sensitivity to contaminating influences that would tend to dilute its faith. It is this which is behind the aversion to intermarriage and the sharp separation enjoined by post-exilic prophets like Ezra and Nehemiah, besides the competition for scarce land and resources during their time.[5]

As has been noted, however, this divide between the sojourner's entitlement to human and civil rights and his exclusion from the faith inheritance of Israel is neither absolute nor permanent.

If he wants to, the resident alien may keep the Passover. But he and his household will need to be circumcised as part of their rite of passage. Even races traditionally regarded to be enemies of Israel can hope to be part of its faith. The children of sojourning Edomites and Egyptians may be allowed to enter the assembly of the Lord by the third generation (Deut 23:7). In the end, according to Ezekiel's vision of the messianic age, the sojourner will eventually share in the inheritance of Israel (Ezek 47:22–23).

What all this tells us is that there is a place for preserving cultural identity, whether that of the stranger or the native-born. Israel had all the right to discipline everyone within its borders to abide by its values and traditions. At the same time, it had to learn early that it could not impose its religious convictions on the alien in its midst. It had to make concessions to those who did not necessarily share its cultural and religious convictions.

Similarly, a case can be made perhaps for countries who, feeling the threat of losing their spiritual heritage, sense a need to impose certain rules as to how precisely foreigners should behave in their land. This does not legitimize, however, the kind of racism and dominance exercised by majority cultures on ethnic minorities. It is clear from this that the alien in their midst has a right to keep his own cultural and religious tradition.

Sojourners Together

People as *ger* – sojourners – is a central metaphor for describing the patriarchs and the history of Israel. Their identity as well as social distinctiveness is anchored on the reality of their being sojourners themselves.

---

5. Both were concerned, not so much with ethnicity, as with keeping religious identity, cf. Kenton L. Sparks, *Ethnicity and Identity in Ancient Israel: Prolegomena to the Study of Ethnic Sentiments and their Expression in the Hebrew Bible* (Winona Lake, IN: Eisenbrauns, 1998), 325.

The people of God are enjoined to "love the stranger," even as they themselves were "strangers in the land of Egypt" (Deut 10:18–19). This call to "love the stranger" is echoed in the New Testament in the command to show *philoxenia*, "hospitality," or literally *phileo*, "love" of the *xenos*, "foreigner" or "stranger."[6]

This command had for its social backdrop not only the difficulties and dangers of traveling during this time, with inns being scarce, scary and costly – there was also the hardening of Jewish attitude towards Gentiles. That they were the "chosen people of God" had by this time deteriorated into a narrow sense of racial and religious privilege. Scholars say that by Jesus' time, the term *ethnikos*, "gentile," or "pagan" had become classed in the same breath as the tax collector, with connotations of something shameful and disgraceful (see for instance Matt 18:17). To devout Jews conscious of their religious identity, the world is made up of "Jews and the rest."

This strain of cultural separatism and moral superiority showed up quite fiercely in the Judaizers' insistence that Gentile Christians undergo the usual rites of passage and identity markers of what it means to share in the faith of Israel. At the center of the Jew-Gentile social crisis in the Early Church was the Pauline insight that "they who were far off have now been brought near." A Gentile believer is no longer alien, a "para-family" person, *paroikos*, but a blood relative and a fellow citizen in the commonwealth of Israel (Eph 2:19; Gal 3:28).

This historic movement towards inclusion is once again being tested at a time when multi-racial societies, particularly those nostalgic about memories of the old "Christendom," are faced with the presence of minorities unabashedly asserting their religious and cultural heritage in political space. Many find themselves pressed between the broad liberalism of secular pluralists and the narrow jingoism of right-wing political religionists.

That the world has come to our doors presents us with social ambiguities. To see strange cultures flashed on our TV screens or lined up as exotic fare in restaurant rows in major cities makes life more interesting. But it is another thing to see people of all colors competing for our jobs and crowding us out of living space such that we smell their cooking. Cultural distance is not as easily traversed as space. As a communication theorist long ago observed,

---

6. See Rom 12:13b, Heb 13:2a, 1 Pet 4:9 and Narry Santos' discussion on these, "Tagapamagitan," 465–466.

"The physical barriers to communication are rapidly disappearing, but the psychological obstacles remain."[7]

It has been said that understanding other cultures is less a *language* process as a *people* process. Psychologically conservative people tend to fear the strange and the unfamiliar. Without sufficient cultural preparation, casual encounters among people of diverse ethnic groupings simply harden preconceptions into racial stereotypes, and, eventually, prejudice.

Whatever else can be said about the subject of bringing people together, it is at least clear from the foregoing that today's migrants are entitled to universally acknowledged human rights, regardless of their legal or political status. There is to be no distinction between citizen and foreigner when it comes to social justice issues.

In a time of reaction to spineless pluralism, there is certainly a need to defend the right of a host culture to keep its moral and spiritual integrity, however that is defined within its own religious tradition. It needs to be said with equal emphasis, however, that the host country has no right to stifle the religious convictions of its minorities.

The tension between guarding a nation's cultural and spiritual integrity and allowing pluralism in faith and culture is something we need to uphold today as cultures get eroded by the homogenizing forces of globalization or move towards a narrow fundamentalism and monoculturalism.

---

7. See the works of Daniel Katz, American psychologist at the University of Michigan who connected individual psychology to social systems and founded the field of organizational psychology.

7

Living as God's People in Alien Cities

Thus says the Lord of hosts, the God of Israel, to all the exiles:

Build houses and live in them; plant gardens and eat their produce. Take wives and have sons and daughters . . . multiply there, and do not decrease.

But seek the welfare of the city where I have sent you into exile, and pray to the Lord on its behalf, for in its welfare you will find your welfare . . .

For I know the plans I have for you, plans for welfare and not for evil, to give you a future and a hope. Then you will call upon me and come and pray to me, and I will hear you. You will seek me and find me; when you seek me with all your heart, I will be found by you."

Jeremiah 29:4–7, 11–13

What does it mean to live faithfully as people of God in alien cities? Migrants tend to swing between nostalgia for the homeland left behind and the pressure to adapt to their new social environment. Many usually hang suspended between hopes of returning and creeping despair that they may forever be in exile.

The Jews exiled in Babylon likewise found themselves teetering between the hope of imminent return and the possibility of a long and lonely exile. There was the sense, fed by false prophets, that the worst was over and the exiles would soon return to their land. There was also a faithful remnant, who accepted the inevitability of severe judgment in the form of prolonged exile. These faced the practical problem of surviving in an alien land while keeping their identity. There was always the threat of assimilation, not just of a foreign culture, but of foreign gods.

In the following we explore what it means to identify deeply with the city we happen to find ourselves in without losing identity.

Facing the Reality of Exile

Jeremiah became a prophet in 627 BC and supported King Josiah's religious reforms which began in 622. After a time of relative political independence and prosperity under the good king Josiah, Judah quickly declined into empty religiosity and social injustice (see Jeremiah chapters 7–19, 25–26, 35–36). Silent for about ten years, Jeremiah resumed his prophetic ministry after the death of Josiah.

Resented as a "prophet of doom," Jeremiah prophesied exile to Babylon as judgment over Israel. It took three decades before his prophecies began to come to pass, starting with the siege of Judah and the first wave of deportation in 598 BC. Jerusalem finally fell about ten years later, in 587 BC, resulting in a second wave of deportation and the end of the royal line.

This letter from Jeremiah to the exiles in Babylon is part of the biographical material most likely put together by Jeremiah's secretary, Baruch. The letter was written four years after the first deportation, when Nebuchadnezzar took with him to Babylon the young king Jeconiah and the queen mother, along with about ten thousand religious leaders, court officials, craftsmen and artisans.

The letter exhorted the exiles to settle and plant their roots deep: "Build houses and live in them; plant gardens and eat their produce" (Jer 29:5). They were to grow and increase their progeny there: "Take wives and have sons and daughters; take wives for your sons, and give your daughters in marriage, that they may bear sons and daughters; multiply there, and do not decrease" (Jer 29:6).

Instead of separation, they were to stand in solidarity with the people of the alien city: "Seek the welfare of the city where I have sent you into exile, and pray to the Lord on its behalf, for in its welfare you will find its welfare" (Jer 29:7).

It is usual for exiles to sit in the sidelines, to view with sullen detachment and a sense of bitter exclusion the drama of life happening before their eyes in the land where they happen to be thrown.

Quite startlingly, Jeremiah urges the Jews to actively seek ways by which they could bless the city of their conqueror. They are to exercise the one resource no other people have – the privilege of imploring the one true God to rain down good on the land of their exile. The mystery of human solidarity is such that their fortunes are bound up with the welfare of the city, no matter how alien and hateful it may be to them.

There were dream merchants – deluded prophets like Hananiah – who conjured illusions among the exiles that their stay in Babylon will be short and they will soon come home. Jeremiah warns against being misguided by this false optimism: "Thus says the Lord of hosts, the God of Israel: Do not let your prophets and your diviners who are among you deceive you, and do not listen to the dreams which they dream, for it is a lie which they are prophesying to you in my name; I did not send them, says the Lord" (Jer 29:8).

Both prophet and people were indulging in wish fulfillment. Humiliated and yearning for home, they have psychologically slipped into the collective auto-suggestion that the worst is over and Yahweh will soon bring them back. Comments Walter Brueggemann: "The threat to the Jews is that they will be talked out of the reality of exile, invited to deny the real place where they must live their faith."[1]

Babylon, both the historical city and as metaphor for the "world" as an organized system that is hostile and in opposition to God, is a place of judgment for their sins, but also a place for deepening their own unique relationship with Yahweh. It is there, in the land where they have been translocated against their will, that they will be brought to a fresh understanding of their faith, this time no longer tied to a specific territory.

The Promise of Restoration

Along with the exhortation to settle for a long-term stay is the promise of restoration: "Thus says the Lord: When seventy years are completed for Babylon, I will visit you, and I will fulfill to you my promise and bring you back to this place" (Jer 29:10).

Once again, they are being stretched to have faith in God's tomorrow, and wait with expectancy for the promised restoration. They are to be patient, not

---

1. See Walter Brueggemann, *A Commentary on Jeremiah: Exile and Homecoming* (Grand Rapids, MI: Eerdmans, 1998), 258.

with the "inertness of despair, nor the suicide of folly,"[2] but with the clear-eyed acceptance of exile as penance and the quiet hope that at the end of it is mercy:

> *For I know the plans I have for you, says the Lord, plans for welfare*
> *and not for evil, to give you a future and a hope. (Jer 29:11)*

Waiting for the promise of return will take a lifetime, seventy years being the normal life span for that time (Ps 90:10). Even so, Israel's God is not one of those tribal gods whose power and efficacy is limited to the territory they are said to rule. He is sovereign over the doings and the rise and fall of empires. Soon enough, Babylon will fall as predicted, like many empires before it and since.[3] Yet running through the time of exile is the hidden fact that Yahweh is making plans to give Israel "a future and a hope."

Mysteriously, exile can be a means of a deeper return than simply being brought back to the land: "Then you will call upon me and come and pray to me, and I will hear you. You will seek me and find me; when you seek me with all your heart, I will be found by you, says the Lord" (Jer 29:12–13). The experience of suffering and displacement – without king, country, temple or land – will make them grow inward and cry once again to the God they have forsaken.

Jewish tradition says that the Lord's glory or presence was to be found in the sacred tent or in the temple (1 Kgs 8:10–11). God through the prophet now says that he is near and can be called upon even in an alien land. He can be worshiped and found even in exile by those who seek him wholeheartedly. "I will restore your fortunes and gather you from all the nations and all the places where I have driven you into exile, says the Lord . . ." (Jer 29:14).

On the whole, the exiles are to resist both the easy optimism of the false prophets and the bleak pessimism of those who cannot see beyond their present devastated condition. "The counsel to settle in exile is against the popular notion that the exile is short and temporary. The counsel to look beyond exile is against the temptation to despair."[4]

---

2. F. Cawley, "Jeremiah," *The New Bible Commentary*, ed. F. Davidson (Leicester: IVP, 1965), 625.

3. Babylon rose as an empire in 612 BC and fell in 539 BC. Its hegemony lasted for seventy-three years. The time from the beginning of Nebuchadnezzar's rule, 605 BC, to the fall of Babylon was sixty-six years.

4. Brueggemann, *Commentary on Jeremiah*, 260.

But Judah must now decide to seek its future exclusively from Yahweh and not rely on uncertain political alliances (Jer 21:8–10). King Zedekiah and those Jews left in Jerusalem must make up their minds to heed the words of Yahweh and not the promise of a broken reed like Egypt. The alternative is certain judgment – the terror of the sword, famine and pestilence, and the final horror of the city being reduced to rubble – "a curse, a hissing and a reproach" among the nations.

The fate of Israel is a sign to the nations that diaspora is, at first instance, the consequence of idolatry and injustice (Jer 13:24). As Jesus later puts it, "He who does not gather with me, scatters" (Matt 12:30).

"Exile is not simply a geographical fact, but also a theological decision."[5]

Rootedness and Resistance

This letter to the exiles is both a call for solidarity and separation. It is a call for rootedness, for deep engagement with whatever city we find ourselves in. In a time when large masses of people have become globally mobile and fancy themselves as "citizens of the world" with no permanent address, this passage reminds us that we are meant to settle somewhere. We are not meant to be free-floating global citizens, uncommitted to any particular place. Even as unwilling exiles, we are to work for the good of the country where we happen to reside.

While we live in an age of constant flux, we must resist the temptation to live in suspension. Transience is a fact of life, but should not determine the way we will live our lives, the way obsolescence has become so in the things we make and build. Instead, we are to build houses as if we will live there forever, tend living, growing things, and sire children as our wager for the future.

Jeremiah bought land in the throes of the final siege of Jerusalem, a gesture of confidence in God's promise that "Houses and fields and vineyards shall again be bought in this land" (Jer 32:15). In the same way, even while we think that "the world is getting worse and worse," we are to invest even now in caring for the earth that we are told we shall inherit. The future belongs to us; we are primary stakeholders in the kingdoms of this world that are becoming

---

5. Walter Brueggemann, *Hopeful Imagination: Prophetic Voices in Exile* (Philadelphia, PA: Fortress Press, 1986), 93.

the kingdom of our God by the inexorable march of his overruling hand in our history.

At the same time, vigilance is necessary, as it is easy to get overwhelmed and co-opted by the power and authority of Babylonian definitions of reality. Nebuchadnezzar carts away to Babylon Judah's nobility and its skilled human resource – those with expertise in defining the meaning of what has happened to them, like the priests and the prophets – and those with power to rebuild, in wood, stone and iron, the city they left behind.

As we can glean from the story of Daniel and his friends, this is with the intent of subtly assimilating the best and the brightest of the exiles into the culture and religion of the empire. "In as many ways as possible, it was the ideological intent of the empire to talk Jews out of Jewish perceptions of reality and into Babylonian definitions of reality, to define life in terms of Babylonian values, Babylonian hopes, and Babylonian fears."[6]

As the people of God, the Jews were to be pacified and seduced into the glamor and comfort of Babylon as a countervailing force in defining their identity. In resistance to this, the Jewish hope of a future beyond Babylon and the prospect of returning to the land of their inheritance was an antidote to treating Babylon as their permanent address.

Wherever we are, we are told to be at home. As the song goes, "Any place I hang my hat is home."[7] But in identifying with others in our common humanity, we are not to surrender identity. By the grace of God we are who we are, says Paul. And as people of God, we are not to forget who we are and to whom we belong.

There is a place for solidarity, but also separation. For it is Yahweh, not Babylon, who defines our social reality, our future and our hope.

The Meaning of Our Exile

The experience of exile, like the kind many of our overseas Filipinos go through, has both a punitive and a redemptive aspect.

As we have seen, exile is a direct consequence of a nation's unfaithfulness to Yahweh. When people are driven out of their lands to seek a future elsewhere, it is usually a sign that something is terribly wrong with the way a nation is run. It means a nation cannot feed its own people, and has ceased to

---

6. Ibid., 92.
7. A Barbara Streisand song, "Any Place I Hang My Hat Is Home."

be a place of safety and security. People vote with their feet in their longing for a "better country," which may be driven by the need to put food on the table for numerous children, the groaning for justice under arbitrary governments, the search for peace and relief from constant conflict and instability, or simply the desire for better opportunities in a wider world where one can breathe and exercise the full measure of one's gifts.

In the case of this country, the massive exodus of people out of this land is not merely to seek a remedy out of poverty. It is, more fundamentally, our people's response to gross corruption and systemic inequality. A friend of mine once put a finger to this in explaining why he left the country: "It is not easy to start again in another country. But here, at least, if you work very hard you can get somewhere. In the Philippines the system is stacked against you; no matter how competent or how hard you work you hit a glass ceiling when you are of humble origin and have no connections."[8]

The phenomenon of many ethnic groups translocated wholesale in global megasocieties is, at bottom, a sign of gross disorder and dysfuntion in the life systems of the nations they have fled from. People endure the rupture from land and culture, even the separation between parent and family, just so survival is at least ensured.

Exile is a metanarrative running through the sad story of Adam and Eve's banishment, Cain's wandering, Jacob's flight from Esau, and Moses fleeing the Egyptian court and ending up in the wilderness tending sheep. At the same time, Abraham's sojourn in Canaan signals a redemptive thread that from then on runs through the stories of God's people who, while in exile, find themselves placed strategically at critical moments in history.

Joseph rises to power in Egypt and presides over a massive food relief distribution in a critical time of famine in the known world. Daniel interprets the times for Nebuchadnezzar and makes him aware that even he has to know that "the Most High rules the kingdom of men, and gives it to whom he will" (Dan 4:25). Esther rises to the possibility that she has come to royal position precisely "for such a time as this," when her people are in peril from the threat of genocide (Esth 4:14).

Exile is an occasion for soul-searching, for a nation to re-examine where it is failing, such that its people leave its borders in droves. What kind of society drives its people to risk being trafficked and abused or unknowingly used as drug mules just to escape poverty? What kind of world is it that watches with

---

8. The author's conversation with a friend, Bert Quimba, in Seattle, Washington, 1983.

cold, indifferent eyes as refugees flee war-torn North Africa, pile themselves in rickety boats to cross the Mediterranean Sea, only to drown in its waters on their way to Lampedusa?[9]

In the case of Israel, the Babylonian exile demanded reconsideration of what it meant to be the "people of God." It occasioned reflection towards a new "paradigm for self-understanding, and a theological construct for interpreting life and anticipating the future," providing context for the writing of fresh theological literature.[10]

Up to this point, Israel's self-identity as the people of God has been tied up to the land as an important part of the covenant promise. Their story as a nation began and ended with the land as an agent of God's blessing and as context and witness. "A wandering Aramean was my father" was the creed that a farmer bringing first fruits to the Lord recited, conscious that they were once aliens and strangers and were now flourishing in the land that God has given them (Deut 26:5–10).

But in the experience of exile, the Jews learned that the land is not indispensable to the continuance of their covenant relationship with Yahweh.[11] Moreover, scholars say that the exile prefigured an expanded Israel which is no longer connected to a specific territory.[12]

Today, as we see large masses of our people crossing borders, mostly in utter desperation, we may need to ask, "What is the meaning of all this?" From God's perspective, what is the meaning of our "diaspora"? What is its outcome, its purpose for us as a people?

---

9. From January to April 2015 alone, 2,000 refugees have died in the attempt to reach this little island on the Italian coast.

10. Kenneth J. Turner, "Deuteronomy's Theology of Exile," in *For Our Good Always: Studies on the Message and Influence of Deuteronomy in Honor of Daniel I. Block,* eds. Jason S. De Rouchie, Jason Gile, and Kenneth J. Turner (Winona Lake, IN: Eisenbrauns, 2013), 189.

11. Ibid., 212.

12. See Walter Brueggemann, "A Shattered Transcendence? Exile and Restoration," in *Biblical Theology: Problems and Perspectives: In Honor of J. Christiaan Becker,* ed. S. J. Kraftchick et al. (Nashville, TN: Abingdon, 1995), 169–182; and Walter Brueggemann, *The Land: Place as Gift, Promise and Challenge in Biblical Faith,* 2nd ed, Overtures to Biblical Theology (Minneapolis, MN: Fortress, 2002).

8

Remembering Zion:
Longing for a Lost Homeland

By the waters of Babylon, there we sat down and wept, when we remembered Zion.

On the willows there we hung up our lyres.

For there our captors required of us songs, and our tormentors, mirth, saying "Sing us one of the songs of Zion!"

How shall we sing the Lord's song in a foreign land?

If I forget you, O Jerusalem, let my right hand wither!

Let my tongue cleave to the roof of my mouth, if I do not remember you, if I do not set Jerusalem above my highest joy!

Psalm 137:1–6

Mass migration in our global world, whether voluntary or forced, has meant the displacement, and eventually estrangement, of large masses of people from their homelands. The hidden story of the pain of exile, especially for those conscious that their identities have been submerged in the multi-racial societies of global centers, living in the margins and consigned to inhabit the "underside of history," has yet to be told in full measure.

In the following psalm we try to hear the heart cry of at least one exile, and how it resonates in our own contemporary context as a nation that has suffered oppressive powers and is experiencing our own diaspora on a massive scale.

By the Waters of Babylon . . .

This song has the feel of a lamentation, with memories of Israel's exile stirring the poet into expressions of resolve not to "forget" Zion. Towards the end, the remembrance of Israel's humiliation inflames him to the point of uttering a prayer of imprecation against its enemies – the Edomites and Babylon.

"By the waters of Babylon, there we sat down and wept . . ."

Flowing from the Tigris and the Euphrates were waters that irrigated the fertile Babylonian plains. On the banks of these rivers the Jewish exiles wept. The sharp contrast in scenery moved them to remembrance of their native land. The bowed-down willows abounding near the streams were fit companions to their loneliness and silence. On the willows they hung their lyres, a gesture of mute defiance. Before their captors who tauntingly demanded entertainment, they would not sing the joyful songs of their native land.

"How shall we sing the Lord's song in a foreign land?"

Those songs were for celebrating Yahweh and his mighty acts in their history as a nation. They would not sing them in a land that was hostile and alien to his ways. The nation and the temple were gone, and with them the joyful celebrations of a people conscious of a self-identity rooted in the land and the memory of what God has been in their history.

The experience of humiliation, of being uprooted from the land and all they hold dear, brings a penitential sense of what had been lost. They were a people without a country. Their religious identity had been shattered by the ravaging of the temple – symbol of their faith, destiny and national significance.

"If I forget you, O Jerusalem, let my right hand wither!"
  "Let my tongue cleave to the roof of my mouth, if I do not remember you,
  If I do not set Jerusalem above my highest joy!"

The psalmist is homesick. In his mind, capitulation to the heathen culture that surrounds them is forgetfulness of his lost homeland. So he vows to remember. The poet utters an imprecation even against himself if he ever lets Jerusalem, seat of Israel's faith, slip from his memory. Let the hand that plays the lyre dry up like a withered stump, he says. Let the tongue that sings praises roll up and be forever silenced if Jerusalem ceases to be focus of the psalmist's joy.

Such was the intensity of this Jew's identification with his distant homeland and its lost spiritual heritage.

Imprecations against Babylon

Fervent grief over Israel's affliction leads the psalmist to utter an imprecation against Babylon as oppressor and Edom as abettor of its ruin. The twisted hostility of a brother-people, the Edomites, left a sting that rankled.

The poet sought healing in the act of laying before God the burden of the memory that continues to sear him:

> "Remember, O Lord, against the Edomites the day of Jerusalem,
> How they said, 'Raze it, raze it! Down to its foundations!'"

Likewise, he prays requital for Babylon, the "devastator":

> "Happy shall he be who requites you
> With what you have done to us!
> Happy shall he be who takes your little ones
> And dashes them against the rock!"

Psalm 137:7–9

The tone of bitter vengeance in these last verses makes us recoil, conscious of something that doesn't quite fit our religion of grace and postmodern notions of plural civilizations. Yet in its wild cry for cruel vengeance, we sense a primitive, human longing for redress, an anguished crying out for justice. For the terror of "what you have done to us," the psalmist clamors for an eye-to-an-eye penal destiny for Babylon. Its women's children are to be dashed to pieces, perhaps in order that a new generation may not be raised up, to wreak anew its devastating dominion over the world.

Such harsh words stop us. They put before us the stark and stringent demands of justice. They also surface for us the very human quality of our zealousness for "Zion," – or whatever it is that symbolizes our identification with what we sense to be connected with the things of God.

In his cry for retribution and the vindication of Zion, the psalmist echoes for us our own wounded longing for rightful redress and the breaking down of systems that oppress us in this world. Something in us understands the howling wildness of it.

Concededly, such zeal for the cause of Zion is not unmixed with the bitterness that comes from having drunk the dregs of the humiliation of being a captive people. We hear in this the cry of someone who has gone down to the depths, that place where the experience of brutal victimization and sheer anguish makes us lash out blindly in hopeless, heedless rage.

Hearing the Pain of Exile

This psalm is a reminder to us that there are those among us who have been emotionally impaired by a wounded history, who speak harshly from a well of bitter experience.

Often, in the din and clamor of protest against the ancient ills that rile us, we detect voices that sound like hard knights of justice. Before it gets our backs up, we ought to remember that very likely, they speak as victims. The screams we hear come out of the hollows of a lacerated soul.

It is conventional wisdom for those of us who sit comfortably in our pews to talk of biblical "balance." We tend to judge those who rant and bellow and annoy us with their social justice passions as somewhat obsessive and unstable. Yet the experience of injustice is such that it does make people rise to fever pitch. It is only those who do not feel enough indignation over oppression and victimization, or who have not suffered injury from first-hand experience of cruel powers, who can afford to talk of balance.

Separated by time and cultural distance, I cringe at the psalmist's vengeful imprecations over Babylon. Yet, perhaps like most modern people, it is only because I do not know enough of what it means to belong to "Zion," to have lost a homeland that is tied up, not just with one's sense of nationality, but also with one's religious identity.

No Chosen People

Since Israel as a nation was identical with God's people in biblical times, it would be stretching it too much to directly liken this heartsick, reverential longing for the land God has given ancient Israel to our own feeling of simple patriotism in our own time.

No nation can lay claim to being "God's chosen," a civilizing "light to the nations," as Great Britain and the United States of America once felt about themselves, with their propaganda of the "white man's burden" and "Manifest Destiny" as thinly-veiled guises for imperialism.

It is always dangerous when a nation claims to be a proprietary heir to God's promises. White South Africa used to rule by whiplash its millions of blacks by legitimizing it as a consequence of the "Hamitic curse," echoing the promise behind Exodus: "This land is mine, God gave this land to me." The kind of national romanticism which found expression in such horrors as Hitler's exaltation of the German "Volk" has no place in a kingdom without borders, where barriers of race, gender and class are dismantled in Christ (Gal 3:28).

Israel itself – the present secular state carved out of Palestine in 1948 – cannot lay claim to being continuous with the ancient nation of Israel as the "chosen people of God." "Israel" as a construct of what it means to be the "people of God" ceased when it was destroyed as a nation. Starting from the fall of Jerusalem in 586 BC, and all through the time of Jesus till the final destruction of Jerusalem and the temple in AD 70, the spiritual "descendants of Abraham" were increasingly distinguished and dissociated from merely ethnic Jews.

It is significant that in primeval history, before Genesis 12, Israel was not in the Table of Nations, or at least did not figure prominently as the center of the nations. It was represented by a name completely neutral – Arpachshad.[1] "The line from primeval time does not lead lineally from Noah to Abraham, but it first opens into the universe of the international world."[2]

It would seem that once again, Israel takes its place as merely one among the nations. While "salvation is of the Jews," its historic role as bearer of blessing to the nations has passed to the churches in those nations. But as a paradigm of God's moral requirements on the rest of the nations, the story of ancient Israel remains cogent.[3]

Israel was vomited out of the land – locus of the covenant promises – for its gross idolatry and social injustice, violations of the Law as summed up in "love of God and neighbor." Instead of relying on God, its sense of national security and self-identity got too wrapped up in the mystique of election and the uniqueness of its religion. The prophet Jeremiah gave voice to this when he warned the Jews of his day: "Thus says the Lord of hosts, the God of Israel, amend your ways and your doings, and I will let you dwell in this

---

1. Comments Von Rad: "That means Israel did not simply draw a direct line in time from the primeval myth to herself. This lineal connection with the myth is the essence of polis religion, where the specific political community can only take itself seriously." A typical list of old Babylonian kings begins: "When kingship came down from heaven, the kingdom was in Eridu . . ." *AOT*, 147; *ANET*, 165. Inclusion of this table means a radical break with myth.

2. Von Rad, *Genesis*, 145.

3. Cf. Exodus 19:5–6. For an elaboration of this paradigmatic approach, see Wright, *Walking in the Ways of the Lord*, 33.

place. Do not trust in these deceptive words: 'This is the temple of the Lord, the temple of the Lord, the temple of the Lord'" (Jer 7:3–4).

This mantra, recited by the false prophets, lulled Israel into thinking that Babylon could not overrun the nation as long as the temple – symbol of God's presence – stood in the midst of them. The triple repetition suggests that superstition and magic had been attached to the temple in the popular mind.

But God is no respecter of religious institutions, even those set up for him. Shiloh once served as religious center for the tribes at the tail end of the time of the judges. The ritual significance of the Ark, however, could not prevent the destruction of the city and its sanctuary during the Philistine wars. Similarly, the temple was razed down to the ground when Jerusalem was sacked.

Anthropology has a name for this confusion of the "things of God" for God himself. It is called "extension transference" (ET), the subtle shift towards regarding the "extensions" or the cultural elaborations of a thing or an idea as if they were the thing in itself.[4] The ancient name for this is simply "idolatry." The institutional extensions round the cult of Yahweh, like the temple or the sacrificial system, have become substitutes for God himself and his ethical demands.

Like Israel, a nation may have for its cultural capital memories of God's gracious dealings in its history. But this in itself does not guarantee immunity from judgment when we forget his ways. Much of the poverty and ills of this country, for instance, can be traced to the sorry lack of public justice and righteousness. This in spite of five centuries of being the "only Christian nation in Asia," and being touted in global surveys as one of the most religious in the world.

The Power of Memory

We cannot help but feel envy at the deep sense of humiliation that the Jewish exiles felt as expressed in this poem. How many Filipinos mourn enough the fact that we continue to be virtual slaves, "hewers of wood and drawers of water" not just for the world, but even in our own land, second-class citizens

---

4. See the works of the American anthropologist Edward Hall, particularly his third book, *Beyond Culture* (1976) which is notable for having developed the idea of "extension transference"; that is, that humanity's rate of evolution has and does increase as a consequence of its creations, that we evolve as much through our "extensions" as through our biology.

to those white gods who lord it over our pockets and our very skies and air space?

Our anthropologists have long observed a characteristic peculiar to our people: "reverse ethnocentrism." While nations like China think they are the "Middle Kingdom," the center of the world, Filipinos think we are but a tiny cluster of small islands on the sidelines, always overrun by great powers and in the margin of all that is significant happening in the world. We have been "inferiorized," thinking that what is "stateside" or foreign is always better than what we have or can ever produce.

It is worth noting that Britain is about the same size as this country, yet it calls itself "Great" and its poets sing of it as a "sceptered isle."

The Jews, even in exile, knew the power of refusal: "How shall we sing the Lord's song in a foreign land?" In a later setting, we find the same intransigence in the singular life of one man: "We piped to you and you did not dance" was the petulant cry of complaint against Jesus in his time. In our case, we not only keep dancing, but our elite gladly go a-whoring for the interest of our foreign overlords.

Some time ago, an American journalist, from a very brief visit and cursory acquaintance with the country, peremptorily declared that ours is a "damaged culture." This is true perhaps for the Filipino elite, those who, like the Sadducees of Jesus' time, have substituted allegiance to Rome for loyalty to God, in exchange for privileges under the colonial government. It is certainly not true with those at the bottom of our cultural divide – the masses of people who have happily remained themselves through all the colonial influences that we have had to navigate.

Cultures that have undergone colonialism tend to display, in varying degrees and forms, maladaptations.

The Arabs got frozen in time, nostalgic over the decayed grandeur of the Ottoman Empire, which they are now trying to revive in such forms as the ISIS vision of a global caliphate as imagined from an idealized past. The Filipinos, naturally hospitable and welcoming of strangers, got unduly accommodative of exploitative foreigners. This accommodative nature has been so taken advantage of that we now have become inured for having endured oppression for so long. Of all peoples, we have this strange capacity for long-suffering acquiescence to unjust treatment, both from aliens and our own political and social elite.

Not so the Jews. They would not sing their songs as cheap entertainment for their captors. Dispersed in exile, they would yet cling to their historical memories and the traditions that keep alive the best of who they are and what they believe. It is not to be wondered at that through centuries of diaspora, the Jews have kept their identity. Drawing from a deep well of memory, they have remained a race apart, able to survive prejudice, pogroms and genocide.

In this period of our own diaspora, I wonder if the millions of Filipinos scattered abroad in all corners of the world have the same passion to "remember," the same deep identification with their homeland, and the same grief and lamentation over the prostrate fortunes of our people.

9

A Vision of a New Economy

*For behold, I create new heavens and a new earth; and the former
things shall not be remembered or come into mind . . .*

*No more shall there be in it an infant that lives but a few days, or
an old man who does not fill out his days, for the child shall die a
hundred years, and the sinner a hundred years old shall be accursed.*

*They shall build houses and inhabit them; they shall plant vineyards
and eat their fruit.*

*They shall not build and another inhabit; they shall not plant and
another eat; for like the days of a tree shall the days of my people be,
and my chosen shall long enjoy the work of their hands.*

They shall not labor in vain or bear children for sudden terror . . .

Isaiah 65:17–25

Globalization has intensified the crisis of paradigm brought about by the collapse of socialism and the dazzling rise of free market economics. Old-time capitalism, displaying a startling capacity for reinventing itself, has not only managed to win the ideological war against planned economies and welfare systems. It has also persuaded us to leave the plight of the poor to the mysterious operations of the market.

It has inaugurated a new era of economism, where we capitulate to the compelling force of economics as a way of solving, not just questions of growth, but issues of poverty, equity and political stability.

How are we to look at the ascendancy of the market as a shaping force in today's societies? What is its place within the economy of the kingdom? What does the Word have to say to us in the face of increasing disparities and gross disproportions in wealth within and among nations?

The following is a look into how these complex questions may be approached from the paradigms available to us in Scripture.

The New Mask of Mammon

From out of the rubble of the Berlin Wall, voices like that of Francis Fukuyuma were once raised prophesying the "end of history."[1] The old ideological battles are over, he said. What we are seeing is the triumph of liberalism, both economic and political. All that we are left with is the boring technical task of tinkering with systems and making economies grow.

Twenty-five years later, the promise that prosperity will be best served by laissez faire economics or by the inexorable extension of economic freedom has proven to be illusory. "Free markets have not only enlarged the gap between rich and poor, but reduced average incomes across developed and developing worlds."[2]

Likewise, the correlative idea that a globalized market will "lift all boats" has yet to yield evidence in the face of the pauperization of large masses of people in both the North and South. Mostly, it has merely seen the rise of a "global middle class" whose consumption patterns are more or less homogenized – laptops, iPhones, fancy hotels and a peripatetic lifestyle that runs up a huge carbon footprint across the skies – facilitated by access to the interconnectedness afforded by global media technologies and the market. This is the elite professional classes who comprise roughly 30 percent of people in today's emerging economies. Experts estimate that 70 percent of the population within and among nations will be excluded from this process.

A new feature of the economic landscape is this undue enthusiasm over the capacity of market forces to induce social wellness. This is the collective unconscious behind even well-meaning efforts to reduce poverty, like microfinance.

---

1. As Francis Fukuyuma explains it, the Western "idea" has triumphed, there is "a total exhaustion of viable systematic alternatives to western liberalism . . ." and we are at "the end point of mankind's ideological evolution and the universalization of western liberal democracy as the final form of human government. . . . The end of history will be a very sad time. The struggle for recognition, the willingness to risk one's life for a purely abstract goal, the worldwide ideological struggle that called forth daring, courage, imagination and idealism, will be replaced by economic calculation, the endless solving of technical problems, environmental concerns, and the satisfaction of sophisticated consumer demands." See his article, "The End of History?" *The National Interest*, Summer 1989.

2. See the critique of Tim Stanley and Alexander Lee, "It's Still Not the End of History," *The Atlantic*, 1 September 2014.

With micro-lending as an initiating instrument, the poor are introduced into the ways of the market, and the unconscious assumption behind this is that they should be pretty much left to subsist on their own. A kind of social Darwinism is taking place, where the spoils go to those who are best able to adapt to the market. Those who can fit into the system survive, while the rest are swept to the sidelines.

The refusal to bail out those who are failing in life – "no free lunch" – is in direct contrast to the intentional legislation we find in Scripture towards securing the welfare of the "poor, the widow and the orphan," those who are most vulnerable and not likely to be able to "pull themselves up by their bootstraps," as former Prime Minister Margaret Thatcher once put it.

There are laws to safeguard the rights of the poor and those especially vulnerable to perversion of justice – like the sojourner, the widow and the fatherless (Deut 24:17). At the same time, special attention is given to providing for the poor who are dependent on the gleanings left after a harvest of grain, olives and grapes (Deut 24:19–22). Slaves when freed are not just sent away empty-handed, but stocked up with sheep, grain, and wine so they can start again (Deut 15:13–14; 23:15–16).

Economic relations, like lending, are regulated in such a way that humanitarian protocols are observed: "No man shall take a mill or an upper millstone in pledge," for these are implements necessary for subsistence (Deut 24:6). Likewise, one may not seize an article pledged as surety but delicately request for it: "When you make your neighbor a loan of any sort, you shall not go into his house to fetch his pledge. You shall stand outside, and the man to whom you make the loan shall bring the pledge out to you" (Deut 24:10–11). And if he is a desperately poor man who has nothing to pledge but the cloak on his person, it should be returned to him by sundown so that he may sleep in it (Deut 24:13; Exod 22:26).

Old Testament law prohibits the exaction of interest if the loan is for a fellow Israelite who is poor and needy. "You shall not lend upon interest to your brother, interest on money, interest on victuals, interest on anything that is lent for interest" (Exod 22:25; Lev 25:35–36; Deut 23:19–20). While the Jews may lend at interest to foreigners, who presumably are mostly traders and the transactions are very likely for commercial purposes, they are not to take interest on any loan incurred by a fellow Israelite that is *occasioned by need*. The law is clear: human need takes priority over profit or business interest.

It is also clear that while Jewish society has been gifted with enough resources, both physical and moral, such that there need not be any poor among them, the sad reality is that the poor will never cease out of the land, a fact echoed as well by Jesus: "the poor you will always have with you" (Deut 15:4–6, 11; compare Matt 26:11). Therefore, says Moses, "You shall open wide your hand to your brother, to the needy and to the poor in the land." The persistent fact of the existence of the poor is not an excuse to not do anything about it. Instead, it is a permanent call for compassion and generosity.

These days, there is a certain fatalism about our capacity to direct immense economic forces towards growth that makes for a more equitable social order. Certainly, we cannot go back to the old welfare systems, which have proven to be not only unsustainable but injurious to human initiative and enterprise. Part of our respect for human dignity is that we make it possible, as far as we are able, for people to make a living out of the labor of their hands.

However, we cannot countenance the massive exclusion of the poor from the wealth that is now being created, whether as participants or as sharers in the global redistribution of wealth. Besides the increased inequality, we have yet to factor in the psychological and social devastation caused by the fallout of poverty and unemployment on self-worth, identity and sense of meaning and purpose in people. Our economic system must be such that it builds on instead of damages the image of God in us.

We need, for instance, to resist the phenomenon of the "precariat" – like our nocturnal cyber slaves draining away their youth in BPOs, this burgeoning labor force that is without tenure, without benefits and shuffled about in short-term contracts outsourced from somewhere. For our society to survive as a viable habitation, we must invent alternative market mechanisms that ensure security, just wages and humanized working conditions that honor commitment between employer and employee and other such ties as loyalty and friendship in the workplace rather than merely transient transactional arrangements.

As in Old Testament times, some safety nets for those at the edges of life need to be put in place. As well, there should be institutional restraints against huge monopolies in information technologies and the unbridled greed and power of global corporations that overrun small local businesses. This regulative task on behalf of the common good is what the state is for. Government exists, not to be in business, but to ensure a level playing field where those sectors who are gifted and mandated by God to do so can grow the economy, employ our people and make them thrive in their own land.

We need to find a way of making our economy grow while having at the center of our vision the plight of the poor. We cannot surrender the future to a market-led social order where the only questions that matter have to do with the bottom line of profit and loss.

"Every Man under His Fig Tree"

Central to the redemptive plan of God is the land. Creation groans, and in response God set into motion the redeeming of the land. From the time of Noah, whose name means "comfort," or "rest," the renewing of the land has been underway. This longing for the lifting of the curse found certain assurance in the rainbow as sign as well as in the Abrahamic covenant. In the end, we are told, the promised land of "milk and honey" is not just for Israel, but for the nations; it is both particular and universal.[3]

"Behold, I create new heavens and a new earth," prophesied Isaiah 65:17. The earth and the unclean works that are upon it shall be burned up, according to Peter. But in its place shall be a new earth that the people of God will in fact inherit. It is not some ethereal heavens but the hard ground of a transformed earth that we are destined to inhabit.

> The consistent biblical hope from Genesis to Revelation is that God should do something with the earth so that we can once again dwell upon it in "rest" with him. The Bible speaks predominantly of God coming here, not of us going somewhere else.[4]

This earthy materialism in the Christian faith is an important frame for our social behavior.

Land as locus of God's salvific action means that we care for the earth. In particular, in a time when people long to feel the earth beneath their feet and confuse the virtual for the real, we are to heal the rupture between land and people caused by modernization, and which is now being exacerbated by globalization.

Isaiah's vision of a new economy is the exact opposite of what is happening in the economies of poor countries today: "They shall build houses and inhabit them; they shall plant vineyards and eat their fruit. They shall not build and another inhabit; they shall not plant and another eat . . ." (Isa 65:21–22).

---

3. Wright, *Old Testament Ethics*, 155.
4. Walter Kaiser, *Toward Old Testament Ethics* (Grand Rapids, MI: Zondervan, 1983), 187.

The first time I traveled out of the country was as a young person on a goodwill tour mission to Japan. I remember how I was struck quite forcefully then by how odd it was that the best of the produce of our land never gets to be seen in our market stalls but instead gets exported and consumed by people somewhere else. Over *sake* and a beautiful dinner table laden with fat prawns and thinly sliced sashimi, I remarked to my Japanese host how fresh and succulent the seafood was. "Where do you get them?" I said. "Oh, that comes from your country," he said. Later, my attention was caught by the juicy watermelons and the flawless skin of the orange yellow bananas piled artfully in the fruit bowl. "You really have nice things here," I said. "Our bananas at home are not as good as this." My host knit his brow in slight puzzlement. "Oh? But these bananas come from the Philippines."

At the end of the dinner, I felt a slow burning inside, and I do not think it was just because of the *sake*. It was the realization of a strange sense of deprivation, that my people back home who produce all that good food out of our land do not even get to eat the fruit of their labor.

There is something very wrong when a farming country like ours gets its rice from Vietnam, its chicken from the far-away US, milk and beef from Australia, and even its garlic from Taiwan. Behind this is the belief that this is the way globalization rationalizes and makes efficient the supply and demand of goods in the world. The best producers beat the competition, the inefficient ones die out. This, however, does not take into account the systemic inequalities that spell a world of difference in competitiveness between a dirt-poor farmer in a poor country who is subject to cartelized pricing by unscrupulous traders and a farmer, say, in the American Midwest who enjoys government subsidies.

Moreover, there is something about the relationship between land and people that not only shapes the economy but determines the pattern by which the very fabric of our humanity is uniquely woven and we all become diverse.

Paul in his speech to the Athenians at the Areopagus gives us a hint on why this is so: ". . . and he made from one every nation of men to live on all the face of the earth, having determined allotted periods and the boundaries of their habitation . . ."[5] This says to us that while we were made "from one man" – there is a kind of humanity that is shared by all – there is

---

5. Scholars say this could be rendered either "from one he made every nation of mankind dwell on the face of the earth," or "from one he made every nation of mankind, to dwell on the face of the earth," Acts 17:26.

a purposiveness in the allocation of territories that brought forth the nations and their peculiarities.

We may infer from this that cultural uniqueness was hammered out of the peculiar contours and features of each people's landscape. What people eat depends on what can grow. How people weave and wear clothes and build houses is determined by climate and materials available in the environment. How people do commerce is shaped by the values attached to the resources that a community deems necessary for survival.

It is this body of unique social habits, life patterns and values developed through centuries which is under threat by the homogenizing forces of globalization.

That certain "boundaries" were set may mean that there are limits, not just to territoriality, but to the range of "habitations" or lifestyle patterns possible. Dietary patterns, for instance. Perhaps it is not to be wondered at that children in this country now become diabetic and hypertensive with the shift from native *kakanin* to hamburgers. We are islanders whose bodies are meant to be primarily nourished by fish in the sea, not by cows in huge pasture lands that eat up space and suck up water.

It is important to recognize that food is not just food; it carries a whole set of assumptions and attitudes on how life is to be lived. MacDonalds is not just about hamburgers, it is a certain lifestyle – food on the run – and comes from a culture whose genius happens to be in standardizing and mass-producing anything through the assembly line. In contrast, it is somewhat hard to imagine that a fast-food chain can be made out of French cuisine.

The industrial age has ruptured the relationship between people and land. Globalization has disembedded goods and people from what sociologists call their "habitus," such that it is now possible to create wealth through the rush of financial traffic in cyberspace without any real reference to the actual movements of goods and services. This disembeddedness makes it possible to amass fabulous wealth – the so-called financial bubble – without having to produce real goods of value.

In contrast, Old Testament law gives us the impression that reification – money in place of actual exchange of goods, property rights in place of land use – can only be allowed to go so far. For instance, the force of the law is that people can have inclusive access to the fruits of the land: "When you go into your neighbor's vineyard, you may eat your fill of grapes, as many as you wish, but you shall not put any in your vessel. When you go into your neighbor's standing grain, you may pluck the ears with your hand, but you shall not put a sickle to your neighbor's standing grain" (Deut 23:24–25).

Those of us who live in more traditional cultures have a similar sense of permission – that we are always free to help ourselves to fruit trees overhanging someone's fence by the side of the road, much like the disciples who felt hungry and plucked ears of grain as they went through grainfields on the Sabbath (Matt 12:1–8).

I had assumed this little piece of economic license was universal, until I went to the UK to do research at Cambridge many years ago. On my way to the college cafeteria was an apple orchard. So at dusk when I went to tea I would happily pick low-hanging apples from the trees and stuff my coat pockets with them. One Sunday afternoon, after a hearty Filipino lunch that I cooked myself, I gave away some of the apples to my party of friends lazing round the garden. Some remarked how fresh and nicely crunchy the apples were and asked where I got them. "Oh, I got them right there, in the gardens of Newnham," I said, quite blithely. Some mouths fell open, white faces turned whiter, teeth half-sunk into the little green apples stopped biting in mid-air. I was told we could all get clapped to jail for stealing apples. It was my turn to gape, aghast that such an innocent infringement on someone's sense of property should be considered a crime.

What I had thought was open access to communal resource was in fact a barred enclosure fenced in, albeit invisibly, by an abstract concept called "private land ownership."

Looking at the biblical material, the communal instinct of our indigenous peoples seems right: no one can own the land but God alone. It does not belong to us; it is us that belongs to it.

What gives us right to the land is the blood, sweat and tears that we invest in cultivating it, in much the same way that our first parents had to expend a great deal of effort in subduing the wildness of the raw earth that was given to them. "*Kabas* and *rada* are strong words of exertion," says Chris Wright. *Rada* is rulership, imaging God's authority over creation.[6]

The right to have a little corner on earth is directly proportionate to our exertion of stewardship over it. It is not some piece of legal fiction like a land title that gives us the right to own it, but the actual care that we give to it.

Needless to say, we can actually cultivate only so much land. Amassing land beyond a certain portion, like the land sizes allotted to the tribes, is more

---

6. Wright, *Old Testament Ethics*, 123.

likely the result of greed and land grabbing, as condemned by Isaiah: "Woe to those who join house to house, who add field to field, until there is no more room, and you are made to dwell alone in the midst of the land" (Isa 5:8).

The Jubilee provision in Leviticus 25 is a structural way of seeing to it that land – at that time the major means of production and measure of wealth – does not get concentrated in the hands of a few landowners:

> And you shall hallow the fiftieth year, and proclaim liberty throughout the land to all its inhabitants; it shall be a jubilee for you, when each of you shall return to his property and each of you shall return to his family. A jubilee shall that fiftieth year be to you; in it you shall neither sow, nor reap what grows of itself, nor gather the grapes from the undressed vines. For it is a jubilee; it shall be holy to you; you shall eat what it yields out of the field. (Lev 25:10–12)

This provision of the law returns property sold before the Jubilee to the original family landholders. Israelites who fall into servitude because of debt or destitution are freed, their debts cancelled, and they return to their families. The land itself shall have rest, a sabbatical in seven-year cycles. To allay anxieties about food security, the sixth year shall have enough harvest for three years – the sabbatical year, the eighth year when the people replant, and the ninth year when the new crop comes in.

The significance of this law is threefold. One, it prevents undue concentration of wealth and holds up the inalienable character of clan landholdings. Two, it emancipates those who, because of some misfortune, fall into debt and eventual slavery and enables them to start again. Three, it renews the land and reminds Israel that the land belongs to God, that they are not owners but only tenants with right to use, or usufruct, and land cannot be sold permanently.

On the whole, the Jubilee is a periodic, structural remedy to economic deformations and imbalances that arise within a 50-year period. It is a kind of social homeostasis, a way of maintaining productivity and social wellness by restoring to impoverished families their original land inheritance.

There is no record that the Jubilee was ever observed historically by Israel. There are references to it in Ezekiel and Isaiah, but these are in a future, ideal context (Ezek 46:17; Isa 61:1–2).

Nevertheless, the vision of an economy where every family has a place, land where every man or woman can "sit under his vine and under her fig tree" in peace and security persists as a thread in the prophetic tradition (Mic 4:4).

Isaiah's vision of a new society likewise includes nature defanged of predatory instincts – "the wolf and the lamb shall feed together" – and people will live long, enough to see their labor bear fruit: "for like the days of a tree shall the days of my people be, and my chosen shall long enjoy the work of their hands." Instead of generational poverty, there will be the blessing of protection and prosperity for the next generations (Isa 65:22–23).

Intimations of a Desired Future

What can be gathered from Old Testament legislation are intimations of what society can be like if the Law were followed. In contexts of highly developed and complex economies, they cannot be taken as literal prescriptions.

However, they hold up to us a social blueprint that needs to be taken seriously in a time when market forces tend to sideline more and more those at the margins of life. Technology has disembedded wealth creation, as well as much of human life, from an organic relationship with the created world. Human dominion over the earth means that we cannot surrender to merely market mechanisms the responsibility of seeing to it that justice and equity are at the center of our vision for growth.

The biblical concern that people should enjoy the work of their hands seems to be the exact opposite of what is happening in this country. Our workers and engineers construct skyscrapers in Saudi Arabia, build infrastructure in Nigeria and train copper miners in Zambia. Yet in this, our home country, bridges and buildings collapse and our power, transport and communication systems are dysfunctional. We train nurses and doctors for hospitals abroad while our rural poor are underserved and die without medical care. Our management experts help businesses in Indonesia, and our agriculturists have helped modernize agriculture in places like Thailand, training farming experts in Nepal and Cambodia. Yet our economy lags behind most of our neighbors and our people are increasingly food-poor and lack food security.

Our women, many of whom are highly educated, tend other people's babies while sundering themselves from their own families, allowing yuppie women of Singapore or Hong Kong to stay in the work force and take off in their careers. In the meantime, our children are growing up in one-parent or no-parent families that are breaking up and increasingly dysfunctional.

There is something very wrong with a country whose main economic strategy is to export its people, along with bananas and pineapples, to faraway lands. While there are no easy answers to going global while remaining local, it is well to remember that overall, God's intention for society is that we get to stay put in one place, to inhabit a land and labor on it and sustain our country and people by the work of our hands.

The emphasis on land is not just pastoral imagery in a pre-industrial age. Land is where we live, a place for sustenance as well as meaning. Our work is meant to be bounded by both its potential and its limits. It is finite, and not an ever-receding frontier for exploration and exploitation. Part of our environmental crisis is this refusal to accept that there are limits to growth, as the Club of Rome in the 1970s discovered.[7]

Land is also that place of "rest," where we go for peace, solace and stability in a time of constant flux and the ever-changing requirements of having to live in multiple worlds. It is where we live real and not virtual lives, as close as we can be to the healing physicality of the good earth that God has created.

The future world, I imagine, is not the gleaming chrome and steel of sci-fi movies that we see. It is an organic city, as pictured to us by John's final vision of the new Jerusalem:

> Then he showed me the river of the water of life, bright as crystal, flowing from the throne of God and of the Lamb through the middle of the street of the city; also, on either side of the river, the tree of life with its twelve kinds of fruit, yielding its fruit each month; and the leaves of the tree were for the healing of the nations. (Rev 22:1–2)

---

7. See the Club of Rome's report, *The Limits to Growth*, 1972.

Part III

Missions in Context: McWorld and the Gospel

10

Jew to the Jew, Greek to the Greek: The Jew-Gentile Social Crisis

Though I am free and belong to no man, I make myself a slave to everyone, to win as many as possible.

To the Jews I became like a Jew, to win the Jews. To those under the law I became like one under the law (though I myself am not under the law), so as to win those under the law.

To those not having the law I became like one not having the law (though I am not free from God's law but am under Christ's law), so as to win those not having the law. To the weak I became weak, to win the weak.

I have become all things to all men so that by all possible means I might save some.

1 Corinthians 9:19–22 (NIV 1984)

We live in a time when our humanity is being stretched and pulled by having to navigate across many cultures. The global world requires of us a great deal of plasticity, to be "Jew to the Jew and Greek to the Greek." Yet the truth is that in spite of the mass mobility, many relate to cultures merely as we would a commodity: we consume them as exotic tourist fare and hang their artifacts in our living rooms as decorative trophies of how widely we have scattered about our footprint. The encounter with strange peoples does not really change us in any way that is significant.

The Apostle Paul, faced with having to cross cultures with the gospel, sets out a few principles on how to relate to various peoples out of his own practice. In 1 Corinthians 9:1–22, we get a glimpse of the overriding concerns behind his struggle to make the gospel much more than a mere Jewish preserve, a tribal religion kept within the narrow confines of the old Judaism.

"Jew to the Jew," or the Case for Identification

Paul's teaching in relation to culture had both a backward and a forward movement. The backward movement had to do with the problem of relating to Christianity's original context: Judaism. In this we see him accommodating the apprehensions of those of his countrymen who misunderstood his teaching on grace and suspected that he was no longer a rule-observing Jew.

The forward movement was his groundbreaking vision of a new community where ancient barriers of race, gender, and social class are broken down (Gal 3:28). In Christ, he understood that all come to the table on an equal footing, and this meant the breaking down of distinctions that keep people from being together round the person of Jesus.

In this passage in 1 Corinthians, he expresses the willingness to identify with those who are "under the law," – his Jewish compatriots – as well as with those "not under the law," – those from other races and religious traditions who were outside the ritual demands of the Jewish law.

"Though I am free and belong to no man, I make myself a slave to everyone . . ." Previous to this, Paul had been talking of how he had been prepared to lay down his rights as an apostle. He had not taken advantage of his right to take along a wife or to be supported as one who properly ought to receive his living from the gospel (see 1 Cor 9:1, 4, 5, and 14).

Unlike those raised in environments where there is a highly developed language and assertiveness about "rights," Paul was willing to subject himself to the constraints of living among a people whose culture and convictions were not exactly his own. This willing subjection underlies much of his teaching regarding areas of cultural tension, such as circumcision and food sacrificed to idols (see 1 Cor 8; Gal 2; Phil 3; and other such passages).

"To the Jews I became like a Jew, to win the Jews." At first glance, this declaration is a bit startling, since Paul was an ethnic Jew – a "Hebrew of Hebrews" – although raised in a more Hellenistic context in Tarsus. The next sentence fills us in on what he means by this: "To those under the law I became like one under the law (though I myself am not under the law), so as to win those under the law."

A major controversy that rocked the Early Church and served as a landmark in the growth of the gospel was a question that once again confronts us in this age of globalization: "How can Jews and Gentiles – races whose cultural and social orientations are so different – live together as one in Christ?"

One answer to this was the way of the Judaizers. Simply put, they demanded that the Christians of Gentile background submit themselves to "the law," by which is meant not just moral laws like the Ten Commandments but the whole legal system that regulated Israel's cultic and socio-cultural life. In particular, they insisted on certain ritual signs that in Jewish culture were viewed as marks of conversion or of what it means to belong to the people of God, like circumcision or eating only kosher food. In effect, they were wanting the Gentile converts to become, culturally, like Jews, if they were to be counted as true believers in Christ.

Another response to the question was the way of Paul and his colleagues. Early on, Paul understood that "works of the law" does not, at any rate, make people acceptable to God. Paul contended against the rabbinic view that Jew and Gentile will have a relationship with God, especially in the end times, but only through the Torah.[1] To demand that Gentile converts be circumcised or conform to Israel's plethora of laws was to deny the fundamental truth that it is by faith in the work of Christ alone that people get saved (Gal 2:11–16).

The principal issue behind the Jew-Gentile social crisis is the disagreement among believers about the continuation of Israel as a privileged people of God, and the place of its cultural correlates – the importance of the Law, the temple and Jerusalem as locus of its faith. The conflict comes to a head in Acts 11 on the issue of the necessary conditions for the Gentiles, where Peter realizes that the old religious order is now superseded.[2]

---

1. Within rabbinical Judaism, membership in the old covenant is considered salvation, and "Any violation of such loyalty to the Torah, as in the case of believing in a crucified Messiah and a christological critique of the law (Acts 7 and 8) is a threat to the well-being of Israel." Yeo Khiok-Khng (K. K.), ed., *Navigating Romans through Cultures, Challenging Readings by Charting a New Course*, Romans through History and Culture Series (New York: T & T Clark, 2004), 9–10.

2. Josep Rius-Camps and Jenny Read-Heimerdinger, eds., *The Message of Acts in Codex Bezae: A Comparison with the Alexandrian Tradition Vol II, Acts 6:1–12.25*, Library of New Testament Studies, 302 (New York / London: T & T Clark, 2006), 9.

The question was brought to the leaders in Jerusalem in Acts 15, which some scholars say is not, properly speaking, a Council, but the trial of Paul and Barnabas concerning acceptance of Gentiles into the Church without circumcision.[3] Circumcision, to believing Pharisees of the day, is sign of belonging to the covenant. Should this be treated merely as a tradition? After much debate, Peter rose, holding up the descent of the Holy Spirit upon the Gentiles as sign of God's indiscriminate grace. "Now therefore," he said, "why do you make trial of God by putting a yoke upon the neck of the disciples which neither our fathers nor we have been able to bear?"

James, a "pillar" in the Jerusalem church who occupied "a position of monarchical authority,"[4] set forth his judgment that the Gentiles were not to be burdened by this "yoke," but were to "abstain from food sacrificed to idols, from blood, from the meat of strangled animals and from sexual immorality" (Acts 15:29, NIV).

"James' solution was both theological – salvific, by grace; and social – how to live together: the double principle of no needful circumcision on the one hand and no needless offence on the other."[5] This was subsequently written down and formalized into a ruling.

The *doctrinal* question about whether the requirements of the Mosaic Law were necessary in order to be saved was decisively dealt with. At the same time, the ruling resolved the *practical* issue of sensitivity to Jewish sensibilities, and how a common table can be shared by Jews and Gentiles who happened to have vastly different dietary habits.

The prohibitions regarding blood, food offered to idols, meat from strangled animals and unchastity are not a "compromise," merely ritual concessions to Jewish fastidiousness. N. T. Wright points out that this is applying the law in context: they may have referred primarily to pagan rituals associated with worship, which involved drinking blood, temple prostitution and orgies.[6]

---

3. Josep Rius-Camps and Jenny Read-Heimerdinger, eds., *The Message of Acts in Codex Bezae: A Comparison with the Alexandrian Tradition Vol III: Acts 13.1–18.23, The Ends of the Earth* (New York / London: T & T Clark, 2007), 11.

4. Acts 13:17; 21:18; 15:13ff; 1 Cor 15:7; Gal 2:9, 12; see Adolf Harnack, *The Acts of the Apostles*, trans. Rev J. R. Wilkinson (London: Williams and Norgate, 1909), 267.

5. N. T. Wright, *Acts for Everyone, Part One* (London: SPCK / Louisville, KY: John Knox Press, 2008), 45.

6. Ibid., 46.

But even when these may not refer, at first instance, to cultic practices, the fact is that something has to give when we come together, some adjustment to what each culture finds unappetizing or downright abhorrent. We are told that in the Old Testament, the term "abomination" denotes something culturally unacceptable. Egyptians find shepherding and eating with foreigners abominable, and so does God on Canaanite worship and sexual practices as listed in Leviticus 18.[7]

Note that together with the sensitivity to Jewish dietary patterns was the intransigence about the demands of moral purity. Chastity was enjoined as a critical sign of conversion, a mark of separation from the surrounding culture, especially for Greek converts brought up in the free-wheeling sexual license of their day.

Christians are to identify and adjust to the constraints of culture as they find them, but are to resist conformity to a moral climate that violates God's norms for society.

The apostles and elders thus affirmed the breaking out of the new wine of the gospel from its Jewish wineskins. This paved the way for the Greeks and other peoples to develop a moral freedom that is within their own thought patterns and spiritual traditions. At the same time, they upheld the limits within which such freedom could be exercised.

Even as Paul was wresting the faith out of the tribalism of its Jewish origins, he was quite ready to be "Jew to the Jew" when necessary. He had Timothy, who was half-Greek, circumcised, because he was to accompany him in places where there were Jews who were likely to be offended by an uncircumcised half-breed. In contrast to this, Titus, who was thoroughly Greek, was not compelled to be circumcised (Acts 16:3, cf. Gal 2:3).

In the latter part of his career Paul was prepared, upon advice of the Jerusalem elders, to undergo rites of purification along with four men who have taken a Nazirite vow. This was to allay misimpressions that "you teach all the Jews who live among the Gentiles to turn away from Moses, telling them not to circumcise their children or live according to our customs" (Acts 21:17–26, NIV).

---

7. Gordon J. Wenham, "Laws and Ethical Ideals in Deuteronomy," in *For Our Good Always: Studies on the Message and Influence of Deuteronomy in Honor of Daniel I. Block*, eds. Jason S. De Rouchie, Jason Gile, and Kenneth J. Turner (Winona Lake, IN: Eisenbrauns, 2013), 90.

Faced with the practical problem of ministering to those "under the law," Paul was highly accommodative and affirming of the spiritual traditions in which he and his people had been brought up.

Greek to the Greek, or the Case for Cultural Abstention

Paul applies the same flexibility to those of Hellenistic background: "To those not having the law I became like one not having the law (though I am not free from God's law but am under Christ's law), so as to win those not having the law" (1 Cor 9:21, NIV).

The Corinthian believers were faced with the practical problem of whether they may eat the flesh of animals that had been sacrificed to idols when invited to feasts by family and associates. The context behind this query was that a considerable part of the meat sold in the market came from left-over portions of the meat offered in sacrifice by the temple priests. Much of this meat was sold to butchers, and eventually found their way either in homes celebrating family festivals or in communal meals with pagan friends and relatives held in a temple and were intimately associated with a pagan deity.

There were times when believers were invited to parties in the houses of neighbors where the meat served had very likely been sacrificed to temple gods before they were sold in the market. Responding to this social problem, Paul tells them that in these occasions, they may eat without raising qualms on the ground of conscience (1 Cor 10:25).

However, Paul says that while he may, as a free man, do everything according to his conscience, he is not willing that this liberty should cause someone else to fall. "All things are lawful, but not all things are helpful," he said (1 Cor 6:12). An idol is nothing, as far as Paul is concerned, for "we know that 'an idol has no real existence,' and that 'there is no god but one.'" In this he echoes those "men of knowledge" who felt at liberty to eat. But while it may be perfectly all right in certain contexts to eat food sacrificed to idols, it is not so when a brother who has yet to be weaned from its ritual meaning is emboldened to eat and thus defiles himself (1 Cor 8:10–13; 10:25–26).

The church in Corinth had both "weak" and "strong" members, referring perhaps to new Greek converts who, in eating such food, associated it with entering into relationship with their old pagan gods, and those who had an enlightened conscience about it and saw it as part of their Christian liberty. These were the "liberals" who saw nothing wrong with participating in temple banquets and as Greeks tended to identify religion with knowledge.

Paul cautioned those liberals who partake of ritual feasts in pagan temples that they may in fact be worshiping demons:

> Consider the people of Israel; are not those who eat the sacrifices partners in the altar? What do I imply then? That food offered to idols is anything, or that an idol is anything? No, I imply that what pagans sacrifice they offer to demons and not to God. I do not want you to be partners with demons. You cannot drink the cup of the Lord and the cup of demons. You cannot partake of the table of the Lord and the table of demons. (1 Cor 10:18–21)

It seems that Paul nuances his permissiveness by making a distinction between sacrificed meat eaten in ritual settings and meat eaten in more neutral social gatherings. The difference in treatment seems to lie in whether the activity is deemed to be morally "indifferent" or belongs to what the Calvinists call the "sphere of the *adiaphora*," or whether it still carries an internal spiritual meaning for the gathered participants.

An approximate equivalent of this cultural tension happens in many places here in Asia where we are surrounded by cultural artifacts that are rooted in religious traditions that rival Christianity.

In India many years back I met some Christians who had been experimenting with the use of *bharata natyam,* the Hindu classical dance. They communicate the gospel to masses of barefoot, mostly illiterate folk through the symbolic language of the dance. I thought then that it was a major breakthrough, hearing tales of how restive masses of poor Hindus could not stand a few minutes of sermons and yet would stand for hours in the rain to watch gospel stories performed by these classical dance artists.

Many years later, I met a Christian who had just come out of a Hindu background. I asked what he thought of the use of *bharata natyam* in telling the gospel. His reply probably reflects the sentiments of those who have yet to come to terms with those parts of their culture that are rooted in the old religion: "I could not stand it. It reminded me of the old sacrifices, the rituals I used to do as a child. It makes me almost vomit."

It is true that things associated with the religion we have left behind can be cleansed and redeemed and offered up to the true God who owns all the earth. It is a cause for rejoicing that the drums are back in African churches, and our folk dances and liturgies, which are rooted in our indigenous religion, are now being reinvested with new meanings and offered up in joy to the altar of Him to whom all things belong.

Yet it is also true that it takes a long time for artifacts of a religious or cultural system to gain new meanings and associations. It took centuries for the fir tree, a feature in Nordic ritual festivals round the winter solstice, to get assimilated within the Christmas story.

Similarly, it will take time and historical distance for cultural isolates like *bharata natyam* or Buddhist chimes and mourning rites to morph into more neutral art forms or transmuted into funerary rites within a more or less Christian meaning system. Until then, those converts who are still steeped in the ritual meanings of the old religion may find it difficult to participate in such activities. Most converts go through an inevitable rejectionist phase about everything connected to their old religion. This is perhaps psychologically necessary and is as it should be.

Behind Paul's exercise of restraint in the use of his own freedom is this voluntary accommodation of the scruples of brothers and sisters whose consciences are still tender and subject to old associations. He echoes this principle throughout, and is perhaps meant to be applied when dealing with both those who are new believers coming out of a Gentile background and Jewish believers who retain the old and familiar wineskins within which they have come to faith. "To the weak I became weak, to win the weak" (1 Cor 9:22, NIV).

For the sake of the gospel, there is this willing curtailment of one's liberty to eat or not to eat and such other behavior which may stand in the way of people knowing Christ.

A Willing Subjection to Cultural Norms

Both theologically and in practice, we see Paul bending over on the side of grace when faced with the challenge of working out its implications within a concrete social situation.

Being under the "law of Christ," Paul was prepared, like the Lord Jesus, to surrender his autonomy and submit himself to the context of the people to whom he had been sent. Like his Lord, he was always ready to "empty" himself, to lay aside his cultural baggage, and subject himself under the norms and lifestyle standards of the people he sought to win (see Phil 2:5–11).

Part of the so-called "incarnational" approach to witness is the willingness to be subject to the structures within which people are to respond to the kingdom. The sinless Jesus went to the river Jordan to get baptized by John the Baptist as a rite of passage and as a gesture of solidarity with a nation that needed repentance and cleansing. John was deferentially hesitant at first: "I need to be baptized by you, and do you come to me?" Jesus answered, "Let it be so now; for it is fitting that all righteousness should be fulfilled" (Matt 3:13–15).

Now, more than ever, we are being stretched in our capacity to identify with whatever races and peoples we come in contact with. To be "Jew to the Jew and Greek to the Greek" requires humility and a certain plasticity, an adaptive power that is possible only to those who are prepared to be subject to other people's norms and values, to lay down their preconceptions, and affirm the life systems of those whose ways of doing things are vastly different from our own.

In a diverse, multicultural world, we are being asked to make an effort to discover sameness, to find a way of being together when face to face with neighbors whose strange customs challenge our own.

In a time of "liquid modernity" and constant flux, we are being stretched, like a versatile Greek actor, to wear many masks, and become "all things to all men so that we might, by all possible means, save some."

11

Communicating Cross-Culturally, or Why We Can Not McDonaldize the Gospel

When the day of Pentecost had come, they were all together in one place. And suddenly a sound came from heaven like the rush of a mighty wind, and it filled all the house where they were sitting. And there appeared to them tongues as of fire, distributed and resting on each one of them. And they were all filled with the Holy Spirit and began to speak in other tongues, as the spirit gave them utterance.

Now there were dwelling in Jerusalem Jews, devout men from every nation under heaven. And at this sound the multitude came together and they were bewildered, because each one heard them speaking in his own language . . .

Acts 2:1–6

Part of the crisis of today's nation-states, whether the megasocieties of the West or the modernizing societies of the East and elsewhere, is the breakdown of a common cultural meaning. In the old days, religious traditions provided a unified meaning system to cultures and served as social glue. This truth has been obscured in secular societies, and is only now being noticed in the rise of fundamentalist religions, as seen in the surfacing of politically militant movements such as the Religious Right in the US, and ISIS in Syria and Iraq and its refurbished dream of a global caliphate.

The rise of modernized professional elites, who unfortunately make most of the decisions in our corporate life, has meant alienation from the centers of power of those vast masses of people who remain within their traditional cultures, which at bottom are religiously-based.

There used to be the notion that the world is "post-Christendom." Now there is the idea that it is "post-secular." In the late 1990s, the sociologist Peter Berger and his colleagues announced the "desecularization of the world," noting the "resurgence" of world religions.[1]

While this may be true of old Europe, which had been secularizing for the past two hundred years, and to a lesser extent the US, the rest of the world has yet to secularize. Many societies, especially Asian cultures, continue to source much of their sense of meaning and point of integration in their religions. This fact has been glossed over until recently, when the Religious Right in the US began to engage the liberals in a "culture war," and the Islamic ummah as imagined by Osama Bin Laden stepped out of the shadows of 9/11.

In the following study, we shall try to respond to the phenomenon of political religions. Related to this, we shall look into the difficulties of social integration and what Pentecost can tell us about being together. Missionally, we shall do a brief study of Paul's preaching in various contexts, and what it tells us about communicating the gospel cross-culturally in a global age.

Primal Identities and Social Integration

The problem of having to live together has always been explosive politically. In the old empires of diverse peoples, efforts at integration took the form of imposing the cult of emperor worship, whether in Rome under the Caesars, or in China and Japan which divinized their royal monarchs.

Till medieval times in the West, that great architectonic structure called "Christendom" glued diverse ethnic tribes and city-states together under one code of faith. In more modern times, the ideology of the nation-state rose to hold together once fragmented feudal fiefdoms and warring shogunates. Often, however, this meant the repression of ethnic minorities or their assimilation into the majority culture.

---

1. Peter Berger, ed., *The Desecularization of the World: Resurgent Religion and World Politics*, a series of essays published in 1999 by the Ethics and Public Policy Center, Washington DC, and Eerdmans, Grand Rapids.

The problem of *social integration*, or what it means to live side by side in multi-racial societies with equity and tolerance, is not new. What is new is the retreat to small communities of meaning – to what has been called "primal identities" – centered round either ethnicity or religion or both. Contrary to the Marxist notion that economics forms the substructure of all civilization, it is in fact religion that determines the shape and direction of people's cultures.[2]

Samuel Huntington's sensing that we are seeing these days a "clash of civilizations" is based on this half-recognized idea. The rise of "political religions," seen in its more obvious form as "fundamentalism," is perhaps best understood as a reaction to the excesses and perceived decadence of western secular liberalism as disseminated by global media.

In the West, the liberal mantra of "pluralism" is seen by conservative people as a spineless surrender to relativism, a consequence of the loss of confidence in transcendence and enduring values. With the coming in droves of migrants, even the idea of "nation" has been eroded as a flag under which people can identify themselves.

An American of Italian descent tells me that as a child growing up in New York in the 1950s, there was great pressure for him and other migrant children to quickly adapt and absorb the "American way of life." Today, he says, you have all kinds of "hyphenated Americans," many of whom refuse to assimilate into the "melting pot" that once was America. As an American sociologist insightfully describes it, "We are now a nation only at work." It is the economic system, not culture nor the old democratic ideals, that now seems to serve as unitive force for such societies.

In the Majority World, it needs recognizing that apart from that thin layer of modernized elites, most people remain rooted, however unconsciously, in their traditional cultures. We see this in the newfound assertiveness of indigenous peoples, and also in the trans-localized migrant cultures that have planted themselves in today's global centers.

Many fear engulfment by rich countries that have massively extended their economic and cultural power beyond their borders. As a form of defense, many are turning to their traditional religions as renewed source of meaning. Militant fundamentalists inserting themselves into political space is partly a function of this reawakened sense of a religiously-rooted identity.

---

2. The missiologist Stephen Neill long ago observed this fact: "There has never yet been a great religion which did not find its expression in a great culture. There has never yet been a great culture which did not have deep roots in a great religion."

The effort to recover a source of integration for the whole of society has unfortunately taken the form of imposing tight orthodoxies based on an idealized past. Religious fervor passes into political prescriptions that in the extreme has become a form of moral fascism.

What does Scripture have to say about uniting diverse peoples?

We have seen earlier, in the Tower of Babel project, one way of going about this: *unity based on uniformity*. A new technology and a common language made possible a large-scale project such as the building of a city with a tower that reaches to the heavens. We see people organizing themselves into a secure, solid society with no need of God.

In contrast, we find in the event of Pentecost a new kind of social integration: *unity based on diversity*, made possible by an interior experience of spiritual power. The Spirit coming down in tongues of fire enabled communication to diaspora Jews and other religious people who had come to Jerusalem from every country in the known world.

Pentecost is an agricultural festival celebrated on the fiftieth day after the Passover. It recalls Israel's exodus from Egypt, their hurried departure following the night of the avenging angel, and their coming to Mt Sinai fifty days after, where Moses received the Law. These memories form the backdrop to its significance theologically. "Pentecost is not just about 'first fruits'" says N. T. Wright. "It's about God giving to his redeemed people the way of life by which they must now carry out his purposes."[3]

It has been noted by a number of scholars that the promise to Abraham of becoming a blessing to all the families of the earth followed the building of the Tower of Babel, the people's scattering and the confusion of their language. At Pentecost, the first-century Jew was witnessing the opposite of these events: God's Spirit was speaking to diverse peoples in their heart languages, and the curse of Babel was being overturned. "God is dramatically signaling that his promises to Abraham are being fulfilled, and the whole human race is going to be addressed with the good news of what has happened in and through Jesus."[4]

God speaks to us in our own tongues. As a consequence of the Pentecost event, three thousand converts were added to their number just on that day. To the Jews at that time, these converts were like the "first fruits" of the harvest that is to come. They were seeing the fulfillment of prophecy in their

---

3. Wright, *Acts for Everyone*, 21.
4. Ibid., 29.

generation, hence Peter's interpretation of the speaking in tongues as a sign of the "last days" as prophesied by Joel.[5] This initial breaking out of Jewish wineskins and its linguistic limits was interpreted as a sign of the Spirit being poured out on all flesh, expanding and universalizing the faith of Israel into a global one.[6]

There is a new, inclusive power at work in the world, enabling not only the ingathering of the diaspora Jews, but also of the Gentile world later. This was prefigured by the fact that as early as 200 BC, it was estimated that there were at least six million Jews in the diaspora – mostly living in Hellenized Roman cities – compared to the one million still living in Palestine.[7]

The event at Pentecost not only refreshed recent memories of Jesus ascending to heaven – "the earth being present in God's sphere" – but also echoed the distant memory of Moses ascending Mount Sinai and going down with the Law. Pentecost was a fresh in-breaking of the "Spirit in our earthly sphere," coming down to us with the powers of heaven.[8] The ability to transcend linguistic and cultural barriers is sign to us of this spiritual empowering, giving energy to the "law written in our hearts."

The dream of a culturally open and pluralized society,[9] based on purely humanist grounds, is not likely to prosper given the natural inclination of most people towards homogenization, as illustrated by the proverb "birds of the same feather flock together." We tend, herd-like, to stick to our own kind; this is why we have difficulty going beyond our ethnic boundaries and usual comfort zones. The dream of a diverse society with a pluralized sense of identity can only happen under the impulse and power of the Spirit of God working in human cultures.

---

5. Ibid., 22–30.

6. To N. T. Wright, the coming of the Spirit and the ability to reach others in their own tongues was the answer to the question of how the promises could be fulfilled: "The whole question of Acts 1 . . . was of how God would fulfill his promise to extend his kingdom, his saving, sovereign rule, not only in Israel but through Israel, to reach the rest of the world" (Wright, *Acts for Everyone*, 28).

7. Rodney Stark, *How the West Won: The Neglected Story of the Triumph of Modernity* (Wilmington, DE: ISI Books, 2014), 34.

8. Wright, *Acts for Everyone*, 22–23.

9. From a conversation with a Dutch friend, who rues the hardening of ethnic boundaries in the Netherlands and in Europe as a whole, and the failure of the dream to be multi-cultural societies that tolerate differences.

Culture-Specific Gospel Themes

The standardizing forces of modernity have tended to shape our own understanding and practice of communicating the gospel across cultures.

We do have a "deposit of the faith," or as Jude put it, a "faith once for all delivered to the saints" (2 Tim 1:13; Jude 3). But the communication of this faith, in the early church centuries as well as now, happens in time and space. This incarnational nature of the faith means that we cannot treat the gospel like a Mcdonald's hamburger, of the same size, same shape and same ingredients wherever it is sold in the world. No one culture or theological tradition can capture its vast density of meanings and turn it into a pre-packaged "simple gospel" that is unduly universalized and presumed to be effective from culture to culture just as in its culture of origin.

Quite early, the problem of communicating the gospel across cultures has occupied the churches since Christianity broke out of its Jewish wineskins.

Men from Cyprus and Cyrene, those anonymous believers scattered by the persecution in the wake of Stephen's death who first spoke to Greeks (Acts 11:20), started to use the word "Kyrious," "Lord," instead of the Jewish "Messiah," in speaking of Jesus. This posed the danger of the Greeks confusing Jesus with such pagan gods as "*Lord* Serapis or *Lord* Osiris." The missiologist-historian Andrew Walls surmises that this must have sent nervous currents of apprehension to guardians of orthodoxy in the Jerusalem church. Much like the way fears of "syncretism" surface when adventurous elements of a church that has sprung from elsewhere do something quite out of the usual theological boxes of the western church. But then, Walls says,

> It is doubtful whether unacculturated pagans in the Antiochene world could have understood the significance of Jesus in any other way. None of us can take in a new idea except in terms of the ideas we already have. Once implanted, however, this understanding of the word received a set of controls from its new biblical frame of reference. In time much of the original loading of the word disappeared altogether.[10]

This interaction between text and context – where the "text" enters the meaning system of the "context," morphs itself within its narrative, and in

---

10. Andrew F. Walls, *The Missionary Movement in Christian History: Studies in the Transmission of the Faith* (Maryknoll, NY: Orbis Books, 1996), 34–35.

time transforms it – is similar to the way Paul engaged various audiences in his preaching.

To the diaspora Jews in Pisidian Antioch, his message is focused round the gospel as something "for the Jew first." He re-tells the story of Israel, moving swiftly from its calling out as a people, to David and the monarchy and the theme of a promised Messiah out of his lineage. "Of this man's posterity God has brought to Israel a Savior, Jesus, as he promised" (Acts 13:23).[11] Jesus' resurrection inaugurates a new age, not just the fulfillment of one nation's longing. The good news of salvation for all the world had come. Paul and Barnabas' turning to the Gentiles is in accordance with God's plan: "Just as Israel had earlier received the word of God, his teachings and commandments, now the nations also receive the word of God."[12]

To the pagans of Lystra, who mistook him and Barnabas as their gods Hermes and Zeus, Paul spoke of a "living God" who made heaven and earth, the sea and all that is in them. "In past generations he allowed all the nations to walk in their own ways; yet he did not leave himself without witness, for he did good and gave you from heaven rains and fruitful seasons, satisfying your hearts with food and gladness" (Acts 14:16–17).

Even without benefit of special revelation, as with the Jews, the rest of the nations were not without witness. This time, Paul pushes the story further back, beyond the tale of a chosen people, to creation and a very big and good God, whose gracious providence fills our hearts with food and gladness. This sermon theme is elaborated in Paul's speech to the sophisticated Athenians. It was a tough audience, for these were people who spent all their time telling or hearing something new, inured to all kinds of intellectual cheap-jacks retailing scraps of second-hand philosophy (Acts 17:18–21).[13]

The speech started innocuously enough: "Men of Athens, I perceive that in every way you are very religious . . ." (Acts 17:22).[14] His violent spasm of

---

11. N. T. Wright notes that unlike Stephen, whose narrative focused on Abraham, Joseph and Moses and the place of the temple and the Law, Paul quickly set forth Jesus as the fulfillment of the covenant promise that a savior shall rise out of Israel and be a "light to the nations." See Wright, *Acts for Everyone, Part 2*, 10–11.

12. Both in Antioch and in Iconium, the controversy was "not just a dispute over the Messiaship of Jesus, but that the word of God is proclaimed as belonging to Gentiles also." Rius-Camps and Heimerdinger, *The Message of Acts in Codex Bezae: Acts 13:1–18:23*, 121, 139.

13. Paul as "babbler," *spermologos* or "seed-picker," is a derogatory term, implying he is a glib gossip picking up bits and pieces of ideas like a bird.

14. The Greek adjective *deisidaimon,* literally, "demon-fearing," is sometimes translated as "superstitious" but scholars say in this case it means rather "reverently devout."

anguish over the city's litter of idols is here subdued into a calm observation of fact. He understood that behind the shrines in every corner, underneath the philosophic polish, is a deep religious longing and a fear of losing count of the gods. The Athenians had to have a shrine even for the "unknown god," and it is this that gives Paul his entry: "What therefore you worship as unknown, this I proclaim to you . . ." (Acts 17:23).

Gently, he introduces a new idea: "The God who made the world and everything in it . . . does not live in shrines made by man." But then he is quick to add something not quite new to the Epicureans, "nor is he served by human hands, as though he needed anything," or to the Stoics, "since he himself gives to all men life and breath and everything" (Acts 17:24–25).

This combination of the strange and the familiar is a pattern repeated in verses 26 to 28. Paul jolts Athenian pride by slashing through the myth of their having sprung spontaneously from Attic soil and stressing their commonality with the rest of humankind. From one man he made every nation to dwell on the earth, and set the limits for their times and territories.[15]

Dimly, in the splendid isolation brought about by a forgotten diaspora lost in the mist of time, there is this human sensing that our ultimate destiny is to seek for God and feel after him. Yet this God who is the unknown cause of our pining is not far from us, for "in him we live and move and have our being," says Paul; we are creatures bound up with his life. These quotations from their local poets Epimenides, Aratus and the Stoic Cleanthes echo the familiar ideas then current among the Athenians and somewhat balance the dissonant note of verse 26.

The following verses, 29 to 31, is a series of ideas of increasing strangeness. In a culture where the gods form the subject of some of its finest pieces of representational art, Paul speaks of a deity that cannot be captured in gold or silver or stone. More pointedly, he speaks of all of that fine art as belonging to a "time of ignorance," a shadowy darkness that God has been prepared to overlook. He then picks up the theme of universal accountability by speaking of a day of judgment before a man whom God has appointed, whose right to it is made sure by his resurrection from the dead.

Such messy talk of a man being raised from the dead disrupts the speech. The people could no longer hear him, used as they were to the tidy idea of an immortality of the soul, or the bleak symmetry of Aeschylus' despair:

---

15. M. Dibelius puts it more philosophically: "He ordered the seasons and the boundaries of their habitations."

"But when the earth has drunk up a man's blood, once he is dead there is no resurrection."

These three passages – Acts 13, 14 and 17 – show that there is not just "one gospel." The themes of a culture determine the text; it frames the message in such a way that it is truly "good news" for that particular people. The Bible itself employed various authors to tell four different versions of the Jesus story.

These passages show us some ways of communicating across cultures, which may be summarized in this way:

- *Find a point of entry as your "text."* Paul connected to Israel's sense of history and destiny by speaking of Jesus as the fulfillment of their messianic hopes. Similarly, the people of Lystra's notion that the chief of the Greek gods and his messenger have come to visit them gave opportunity to point them to the "living God" whose goodness is experienced in creation. The altar with the inscription, "to an unknown God" opened conversation on the Athenians' religious ideas and moved them to the idea of a transcendent God before whom all are accountable.

- *Proceed from the familiar to the unfamiliar.* Paul moves from quoting local poets whose ideas give voice to God's nearness, to the strange and challenging idea that God's being is beyond all human imagining. He then labels their fine effort at artistic representation as "ignorance," and goes on to the need for repentance and the prospect of judgment through a man risen from the dead.

- *Move from affirmation to judgment.* Notice that Paul does not say that the Athenians were "idolatrous," which they are. Instead, in a backhanded way, he commends them as "religious." He went behind the surface phenomenon of so many shrines dedicated to a multitude of idols and saw that these were expressions of a longing deeper than pagan fear. From this affirmation, he then proceeded to the hard sayings.

To enter the story of a culture, we need to suspend judgment until we have fully understood what is behind its apparently outrageous features. We first discover its inner logic, or why people do what they do. Within their own internal meanings, all cultures are rational.[16]

---

16. The missiologist and linguistic scholar Eugene Nida had long ago proposed that all cultures have a logic of their own. Some cultures may have practices that to an outsider may seem barbaric, like burying alive menfolk in their prime. But within the culture's frame of meaning, this may be perfectly rational: they have to be strong enough to still hunt in the afterlife.

In communication theory, there is what is called "cognitive dissonance." Messages that are too negative create in the receiver such internal dissonance that one is likely to seek relief by searching for information that will reinforce one's position or belief. Notice that when Paul came to speaking of the resurrection, the listeners could no longer hear him. Some mocked, and others diplomatically dismissed him by saying, "We will hear you again about this" (Acts 17:32).

Too much negativism or strangeness is counterproductive. In Catholic cultures such as ours, for instance, it is poor communication to right away bash the people's devotion to Mary and the saints, especially among those who see this as constituting the core of what religion means to them. As with so-called "ancestral worship" in Buddhist cultures, to be critical of such veneration is to take away a people's lifeline. Until the lordship of Jesus has become a reality in people's lives, it is premature to pull this magic carpet from under their feet.

There will always be things in the gospel that will run counter to certain elements of any given culture. But we have no right to judge a culture until we have fully understood what lies behind the strangeness or what looks like unorthodox practices. The biblical pattern seems to be that we begin with affirmation before we move to making judgments.

On Deep and Surface Structures

After five centuries of Christianity, Filipino culture remains, at bottom, unchanged. Since the first Spanish friars landed in the sixteenth century, evangelization had been less a Christianizing of the native consciousness as a "filipinizing of Christianity" as a Roman Catholic scholar puts it.[17] There is a complex of reasons behind this. My sensing is that one major factor is the failure to connect and engage the "deep structures" of the indigenous imagination.

One example will suffice. A major theme of western missions, both Catholic and Protestant, is salvation defined as "securing a ticket to heaven." Our indigenous consciousness, however, is profoundly uninterested in the question. We see death as merely a passage to the Sky World, where our dead ancestors live pretty much in the same way they have lived on earth.

---

17. Jose M. de Mesa, consultation on "Hispanic Catholicism and Lowland Filipino Culture," *ISACC Research on Early Protestant Missions and the Indigenous Consciousness, Track 2, Conversion to Protestant Christianity Report, Vol. II, 3.*

An account written by a Spanish missionary, Fr. Valerio Ledesma, in 1601, gives us a glimpse of this disinterest:

> When I was explaining to a fierce and barbarous fellow the great glory of paradise, and the terrible pain of hell, he answered, just as if being possessed by the Devil, that he'd rather go to hell than paradise . . . but I did not hesitate to attack the foolish fellow again and again, and I emphasized to him the horror and the eternity of the torments with great vehemence and language. But he answered that he was certainly going after this life to the place where his parents and the rest of his ancestors had gone, rather to anywhere else. I replied that he had better just try the force of the fire. But he, with hands as hard as his heart, did not hesitate to snatch some burning coals from the hearth.

Similarly, even in this day and age, Filipinos tend to stare blankly at a western missionary when they are asked, "Are you saved?" They are hard put to make an answer because the question has no meaning.

It is important to note, however, that this question has great significance to what the theologian Krister Stendahl calls the "introspective conscience of the West."[18] It summons images of the tortured monk Luther gashing his knees as he climbed the steps of the Scala Sancta, such exertions driven by a guilt-ridden conscience that always asks, "am I saved?" It is no wonder that it was such solace when he discovered those passages in Scripture that told him he is saved by the work of Christ and not by "works of the law."

This Reformation theme was embraced by a small minority of Filipinos at the turn of the last century when the American Protestants came. Those with a reflective turn of mind responded to the theme of "*sola fide, sola gratia,*" mainly in reaction to the abuses of the Spanish friar and as an act of insurrection against Spain. After seventy years, however, a study found that only 1 percent of the mainly Catholic population had crossed over to Protestantism.[19]

---

18. Krister Stendahl, "The Apostle Paul and the Introspective Conscience of the West," *HTR* 56 (1963), originally an address at the annual meeting of the American Psychological Association, 3 Sept 1961.

19. For a fuller explanation of why this is so, please refer to chapter 12 of the author's previous work, *A Clash of Cultures: Early American Protestant Missions and Filipino Religious Consciousness* (Mandaluyong City: De La Salle University Press and Anvil Publishing, 2011), 166ff.

Part of the reason is that Filipinos are mainly occupied with maintaining harmonious relations, both here and in the afterworld, and do not much care for some legal fiction that declares them fit to secure a place in heaven. This gospel theme is not good news in a context where death is not so much an existential crisis as it is in the West, and religion is at any rate oriented, not towards future security, as finding relief from the travails of the present.

Whether we are conscious of it or not, we all tend to *absolutize* our theological readings and understanding of what the gospel is about. Thinking that we are perched from some "Archimedean point of view," we organize our theologies round a motif that we happen to see as important in our context and then foist this on others as "core content," hence the talk about an "irreducible minimum." Theologians have unfortunately inherited a Greek habit of mind, abstracting what we see as the "core" or the "essence" of the gospel, and then assuming that such a reductionist and disembodied formulation will connect and move all other peoples.

In communicating across cultures, it is important to be aware of such "deep structures," which rarely change, if ever, through time. As I have written elsewhere,

> it is not enough to look at what anthropologists call the "surface structures," – things like how people produce food or make their technologies and tools to feed and clothe themselves, how they build houses, eat, marry, raise children, how they transmit knowledge, control and rule their communities, how they relate to other peoples, nature and the supernatural. More importantly, it means inquiring into the "deep structures," into underlying worldviews, a people's way of looking at the world, deep-seated beliefs and value systems that are largely unconscious, and yet both shape and are shaped by the physical and social environment in which the community is embedded.[20]

The passages in Acts that we have studied are good examples of what it means to engage the "deep structures" of a specific culture. They also illustrate what missiologists call "concept fulfillment." This process is perhaps best described by the writer to the Hebrews: "In many and various ways God spoke of old to our fathers by the prophets; but in these last days he has spoken to us by a Son" (Heb 1:1–2).

---

20. From Maggay, *Rise Up and Walk*, 137.

In Jesus, we see clearly and finally the fulfillment of what in many cultures are merely "dark speech," – "shadows" in the language of Hebrews, intimations of an eternal reality beheld dimly by Plato's cave men, or sensed in mythic tales of a dying and rising god pouring out its blood to appease the ancient wrath that has cursed the ground.

12

From Every Tongue and Tribe and Nation: On Being Global and Incarnational

*After this I looked, and there before me was a great multitude that
no one could count, from every nation, tribe, people and language,
standing before the throne and before the Lamb. They were wearing
white robes and were holding palm branches in their hands. And they
cried out in a loud voice: "Salvation belongs to our God, who sits on
the throne, and to the Lamb."*

*All the angels were standing around the throne and around the
elders and the four living creatures. They fell down on their faces
before the throne and worshiped God, saying: "Amen! Praise and glory
and wisdom and thanks and honor and power and strength be to our
God forever and ever. Amen!"*

Revelation 7:9–12 (NIV)

In these "end times," when people are increasingly feeling the power of the
Beast, we are tempted to look at the world as a sinking ship. Like frantic
rats holed up in some dark hole, we just want out – drop everything and "save
souls," – and get everyone to jump overboard, out of this evil world.

It is true that we live in times of extreme pressure. "The time is coming,"
said Jesus, "when anyone who kills you will think they are offering a service

to God" (John 16:2, NIV). I think of this verse when I hear of Christians being beheaded or imprisoned and tortured in many places in today's world.

But then, from the one book that gives us a glimpse of what is really happening in these "end times," things are not as they seem. John draws the curtain that veils the other side of our present history, and lets us see what he sees, which is how the world actually looks from the heavens. In this chapter, we get a picture of the people of God made secure, a multitude without number from every nation, tribe, people and language, worshiping before God and the Lamb who sits upon the throne.

It is not the powers of this world who are at the center of the universe. It is the Lamb, who yet bears the marks of being slain, yet lives and sits from the center of all power.

The following is a reflection on what this means for those of us who fear the "end of history."

Re-centering on the Lamb

This grand vision of the entire people of God worshiping the Lamb at the end of time comes as an interlude between the sixth and seventh seal. The seals are a series of revelations regarding the events leading up to the final coming of Christ.

Tucked in-between the opening of the sixth seal, which reveals the coming of the great natural disasters, and the seventh seal, which paints a fearful picture of plagues and nature conking out, is a glimpse of the Church Triumphant, symbolized by the 144,000 from the twelve tribes of Israel.

Before this vision, we are given a picture of four angels standing at the four corners of the earth, holding back the four winds, that no wind might blow on earth or sea or against any tree. Another angel had restrained them, saying "Do not harm the earth or the sea or the trees, till we have sealed the servants of our God upon their foreheads" (Rev 7:1–8).

In the midst of the terrors of the "great Day of Wrath," we find inserted a glimpse of what finally happens to those who stand fast as they bear witness in tears. We are being told, as it were, that in the teeth of our struggles and the disasters of our time, God is "round about his people," as the Psalmist puts it.

The mark on our foreheads does not seal us from the "thousand and one shocks that flesh is heir to."[1] We are not immune from the calamities that

---

1. The phrase is from Shakespeare.

this country is often subject to – one time reeling from earthquakes, then buffeted by wind and waves such as that brought by the deadly Typhoon Haiyan. Crops suffer drought, sea creatures become inedible by red tide, and the teeming informal settlers precariously perched along waterways become both cause and victim of environmental disasters.

While God does rescue some people in unexpected ways, the experience of disaster and social devastation is universal. Human solidarity is such that we all suffer hardships and political turmoil. What we are sealed from is the awful judgment of God upon sinful humanity at the close of history. Even now we witness the terrible "wrath" that is now shed abroad, at work in the sickness and upheavals of our societies.

In contrast, at the heart of this particular vision of John is the people of God made safe and secure and joyfully at worship.

More than all other occupations, worship decenters our attention from the terrible instability and fearfulness of life and re-centers our vision unto him "who sits upon the throne." We are reminded that "salvation belongs to our God," and it is him who sits at the center of all power.

We worship a Lamb – a "little lamb," we are told in the original Greek. The "Lamb slain," who yet bears the marks of his wounds and of his death reminds us that God knew weakness and paid a terrible price in the hands of evil. The "Lamb at the throne" tells us that nothing happens in the world that is outside of his control. As we worship this God, we become more and more aware that there is no need to be afraid of vulnerability and weakness.

In the face of overwhelming danger and our own powerlessness, worship brings us to a place where we connect with the hidden realities that truly move our world. In its seeming uselessness, worship is a poised counterforce to the frenzied currents in our political and economic life which call to mind the seductive and totalitarian powers of the Beast.

A Great Cloud of Witnesses

Throughout the ages, the people of God have often looked like a ragtag band of eccentric recalcitrants, out of sync with the songs the world sings. Like the Lord Jesus, we get subjected to the same complaint lodged against him by the children of this generation: "We piped to you, and you did not dance" (Matt 11:16–19).

In our time, we may sound like voices in the wilderness, standing in the way of the great social forces shaping this generation. *Laban sa agos ng mundo, sabi nga* – "always against the world's currents," as they say. But this vision tells us that we are by no means marginal. We stand in a long line of witnesses – people who, by their faith and courage, have kept alive the vision of another world present in our midst. While we may not have the eyes to see it, there is an alternative social reality at work among us, premised on the confidence that "the kingdoms of this world are becoming the kingdom of our God" (Rev 11:15).

When the "end of history" truly comes, there will be this great throng around the throne, a multitude described as numberless. We may, in our time, look like mere pockets of hapless believers, scattered about in societies dominated by the world's systems. I imagine this is the way it must have looked to John also, exiled in the lonely island of Patmos in a time of great persecution.

But here he is given a picture of a great crowd beyond counting, a church past the trials and tears of tribulation. It is a people who shall neither hunger nor thirst anymore, led by the Lamb himself to springs of living water. God himself shall shelter them with his presence, and wipe away every tear from their eyes (Rev 7:13–17).

It would be a great pain not to be part of this joyous, multi-cultural throng. Those of us who come from cultures whose main idea of joy is sitting around the table with family, relatives and friends in a great fiesta shall feel it especially when they find themselves excluded from the Great Banquet prepared by the Lamb. The Psalmist depicts judgment as exclusion from "the assembly of the righteous" (Ps 1:5, NIV). There will come a time when the people who refuse to come to the Lamb's feast now shall forever weep and gnash their teeth, wishing they were part of this glorious throng.

A Multicultural Hymn

Of special interest to us is the diversity of this multitude. They were, it is said, "from every nation, tribe, people and language."

The praise offerings that welled up inside them were products of their cultures, sung in their own tongues. While there was only one theme, we could imagine that the variations are infinite: the voices raised are of every conceivable rhythm and language. As in Pentecost, the one hymn of praise shall be sung, heard and understood in their own tongues by all the peoples represented.

In a time when the forces of globalization tend to flatten out cultures and we get persuaded that the world is homogenizing, this vision tells us that ethnicity is not an accident of history.

Our identity as tribes and peoples will not cease. We shall continue to behave as identifiably Filipinos, even as Visayans and Ilocanos, no matter how far-flung we can get scattered about in today's global centers. While national boundaries may shift, as had happened in colonial Africa, or get broken up into more ancient dividing lines of religion and ethnicity, as with Serbs and Croats, Czechs and Slovaks, or wracked by conflict as in Iraq and Syria, or in Sri Lanka between the Tamils and Sinhalese – *peoplehood* as a defining identity will remain.

Notice that "nation" is first in this enumeration of who shows up in this multitudinous crowd. This is slightly different from the earlier verse, "from every tribe and tongue and people and nation" (Rev 5:9–10). In spite of increasing pressure to de-territorialize, political boundaries will still be there.

There is a great deal of talk these days about nations "withering away," this time not because of the old Marxist dream of a universal rule of the proletariat, but because of market forces battering down national borders. This vision shows that "nations" will endure as political units. At the same time, tribal cultures that now get suppressed within an unjust nation-state will find themselves represented. The uniqueness of who we are as "indigenous peoples" will survive the hegemony and deadening uniformity of the reign of the Beast (Rev 13:7).

Going Truly Global

In Revelation, one of the meanings of the mark of the Beast is a standard identity imposed on everyone. The dominance and power of the Beast is such that no one can buy or sell without this identifying mark (Rev 13:16–17).

In the world today there is much talk about the need to be part of the global market economy if we are to do business with anybody. Increasingly, our lives are being shaped by the monocultural forces of globalization, inducing us all to eat hamburgers instead of *lumpia* or *sushi*, organize our day by computer, watch Justin Bieber or whoever is the latest pop icon on MTV, run around town with our smart phones or in general assume the life patterns determined for us by a technologically mediated social environment.

We are not suggesting that the logic of the market or the wonders of technology are evil in themselves. They are to be affirmed as continuous with the mandate to discover the design of the created world and build on it. What bears watching is the way technology and the market have disembedded people from their own worlds, driving us all towards a universalized pattern of consumption and a consequent lifestyle of uniformity.

There is something about the power to mass-produce and standardize, to organize production along simple, repetitive lines, that conjures memories of technology-driven projects like the Tower of Babel. It is not of such stuff that the kingdom is built. The notion, for instance, that the gospel can be standardized into a pre-packaged gospel kit and mass-marketed to many cultures does not quite fit the Bible's own concern for culture-specificity.

Christianity is a *global* religion that is at the same time *incarnational*.

I have never ceased to be amazed that Jesus, the man for all cultures and all times, was a Jew. No other religion speaks of God in this way. Hinduism has this idea of avatars making fleeting appearances on earth, but such flitting visitations are lost in the mist of mythical time.

Jesus, by contrast, can be geographically located. He had a culture and a history that can be pinned down on a calendar – born about 4 BC in Bethlehem, brought to Egypt as a refugee baby, grew up in Nazareth and plied his trade as a carpenter till he was thirty. Then he roamed round Lake Galilee and the hills, valleys and crags of Palestine as an itinerant preacher and healer, and after three years was crucified by colonial Rome in the outskirts of Jerusalem.

The notion that nationality is incidental and the place we live in merely an address is unsupported by Scripture's emphasis on the incarnation as a model of life and witness. We are not meant to be free-floating global citizens – *tipong mga dahon na nakalutang* – but people who, like the Lord Jesus, are rooted in a particular place and culture, with a heritage that we can take with us when we enter the gates of the new Jerusalem.

Being "incarnational" in witness means that we take seriously a culture's themes and construct a culture-specific message that truly speaks to that culture.

The lack of such culture-specificity may account for much of Christianity's unsuccess in Asia as a region. There is a failure to engage the "deep structures" of its religious traditions which rival Christianity in philosophical depth. If, after five centuries, a friendly and open culture like ours remains, in its subterranean structures, deeply unconverted, it is not likely that the rest of Asia, with its consciousness steeped in its ancient religions, would be receptive to the kind of pre-packaged gospel messages going the rounds globally.

In a time of multiculturalism, the growing emergent churches in the South are in a uniquely historic position to refigure the shape of Christianity in their own contexts.

The Latin Americans have shown the way with their liberation theologies and the surfacing of the social dimensions of the gospel as core content. In parts of Asia and Africa, there are ongoing attempts to organize gospel messages round alternate centers of concern, like the cosmic implications of the cross over spirit powers, and the hidden menace and potency that lurks just beneath water, tree or air and other such environmental presences.

Nonwestern churches are decentering theologies from an undue preoccupation with Reformation themes of the sixteenth century, or even with the questions posed by modern rationalism and skepticism.

Most people in this country believe in God, and our indigenous spirituality has never had to contend with the kind of crisis brought about by the upheavals that had rocked Europe – from the Reformation to the Age of Enlightenment to the Industrial Revolution down to modernity and postmodernity. Its main crisis had been surviving its suppression under the Spanish friars, and transmuting itself into an acceptable form, whether as "folk Catholicism" or as "folk Pentecostalism."

It is time we move away from a *transnational* model of mission to an *incarnate* one, with a gospel that is shaped autochthonously.

It needs to be said that there is a difference between *contextualization from within* and *contextualization from without*. The latter is merely adaptation, an accommodation to the surface structures of culture – like putting on Chinese dress or some local costume, fasting during Ramadan, refraining from eating pork or some other form of courtesy to local context. The former, which is contextualization *from within*, is a whole lifestyle and message arising from a thoughtful engagement with the deep structures, the "root metaphors" by which a culture defines and sustains itself.[2]

Part of the mystery of the incarnation is that we are most universal when we are most particular. The God of the universe took upon himself the particularity of a Jewish boy in Nazareth: he was circumcised, played and walked its dusty streets, went to the synagogue and observed all the ritual festivals in Jerusalem, ate kosher food and looked like any other boy of his

---

2. For an understanding of what the author means by "contextualization from within" and "contextualization from without," please see chapter 13, Maggay, *A Clash of Cultures*, 174–191; and my earlier essay, "Communicating the Gospel from Within, Some Culture Themes," in *Doing Theology in the Philippines*, ed. John Suk (Mandaluyong: OMFLit, 2005).

race. All that we know about God was mediated through all that was human about him – "that which we have heard, which we have seen with our eyes, which we have looked upon and touched with our hands" – as John says in amazement (1 John 1:1).

We are entering an age where the "manifold wisdom of God is being revealed" as the Spirit speaks to the rest of the churches. There is a hiddenness to the face of Christ that awaits discovery as his people grow "from one degree of glory to another." They mirror his image through the prism of their own cultures, and consequently surface a face of Christ that has not been seen before. It is when we are most local, most true to who we are and what is given to our natures that that we also reveal something of the uniqueness and universality of Christ.

Quite unwittingly, the anthropologist Clifford Geertz sensed this mystery and gives expression to it in one of his writings: "It may be in the cultural peculiarities of people – in their oddities – that some of the most instructive revelations of what it is to be generically human are to be found."[3]

There is a sense in which we are "global," an interdependent community of God's people all over the world who bear a family resemblance. This does not mean, however, that we cease to be creatures of our cultures, in much the same way that we do not cease to be male and female, rich and poor, even as we are one in Christ. Each local body of believers, in its very peculiarity, forms part of that picture of renewed humanity that Christ is re-creating.

The end of Revelation talks of how the glory and honor of the nations – all the immense richness, splendor and variegated color of them – shall be brought into the new Jerusalem (Rev 21:26).

When the saints come marching in, we shall take with us our *kundiman* and *kulintang*, our flair for color and design, our passion for interconnectedness and the sheer grace and verve with which we celebrate and make us one of the happiest races on earth. These are not simply baggage that will have to be left at the door.

Cultures have an enduring integrity that we do well to guard and keep against forces that would seek to make us all the same. Diversity, not homogeneity, is God's design for the world. Let us remember this whenever we are face to face with pressures to surrender our rootedness and our being "peculiar" as a people.

---

3. See C. Geertz's famous book, *The Interpretation of Cultures* (New York: Basic Books, 1973).

Postscript

The "Prince of the Power of the Air," or Why It Is Time to Put the Monsters at the Center

This morning I woke up rather lazily to soft yellow bands of light streaming through the blinds of my bay window. Through the golden haze I could feel, in that twilight between sleep and waking, the increasing warmth of the sun lapping my limbs, my cheek and the back of my neck, deliciously creeping like a clean tongue of healing fire.

I was dead tired the night before, and slept soundly like a log as soon my back hit the bed. I lay like a sack of bones, only to waken to a light, floating feeling, the whiff of wind faintly stirring the imagination to the clouds and sky outside, where the air is clean and the earth stops us anew with the freshness of morning. I marvel at the miracle of sleep – this silent, wondrous repair of yesterday's wearing – making us whole again in the dead of night. Sleep is a spell that transforms us from what is dead and dying within us to that which is alive and quick, like a flame that flares upon touching the wing tips of a moth.

I try to carry through the day this feeling of a renewing mercy at the heart of existence, an inexhaustible capacity for new life that assures us that we can start again. But then I turn on the radio and hear news of yet another corruption scandal. Fratricidal wars within and among nations, within and among religions, dim any prospect of lasting peace. The promise of bread and freedom, under whatever world order – whether *Pax Socialista* or *Pax Capitalista* – always seems to shrivel up into putrid politics and the mirage of consumerism. My own sense of a world where dreams can hold against the onslaught of disillusionment splinters before the images conjured by the radio.

Yet the plate before me shines and smells with the two halves of *pan de sal* buttered and garlicked and toasted piping hot sitting prettily on it. Morning gold streams through the wide, open windows, casting a sheen on the green plants inside. Something inside me is full to bursting, an "unberable lightness of feeling" welling up into an utterance of joy and praise in the tongue, filling the mouth with laughter. It is as if the bad world could not touch it, could not even come near it, for something pure and holy has descended and claimed me. A flaming sword seems to guard those soft places inside which remain vulnerable to assaults of despair from without. This, I thought, is the *primary reality* – that we go under the protection of God's mercy even as we walk through the shadows of our history.

"A Spirit That Always Denies"

In a time when hope gets frittered away by our own proclivity to fracture and futility, it is easy to succumb to that "something in the air" which fills us with the murky heaviness of despondency. Paul in Ephesians 2 tells us of a "prince of the power of the air," the spirit that is now at work among "sons of disobedience." In an age when our dreams and our very imagination are shaped by the virtual reality conjured by media, this may be the spirit that is at work in those places where opinions are formed, and by diffusion creates a climate, a certain atmosphere that surrounds us like a fog.

It is not something you can nail down or put your finger to. It is something you breathe and feel, an environment that envelops you with a doleful wretchedness sometimes, or with an unaccountable enthusiasm other times. The Germans call it "zeitgeist" – the spirit of the times. We call it *takbo ng panahon* – "the way time runs," or *yung mga bagay na sinasakyan mo dahil yun ang agos ng kasalukuyang mundo* – "the waves we ride on because that is where the wind blows in our current history."

The French sociologist Emile Durkheim has long ago observed that there are "states of effervescence," times when societies seem to glow with exuberance, an overflowing burst of energy that raises expectations that everything is possible. We experienced this in those heady days of our People Power in 1986, when a people famous for fractured efforts organized with astonishing speed a historical venture that was to cause the downfall of a powerful despot.

The exhilaration over our historic potential as a nation rapidly dribbled away, however, into sputtering exertions that looked more and more like a freight train that had lost steam. The consensus among those who burden us with column inches of solemn assertions is that perhaps we are really at the tail end of an economic race that we cannot hope to win among our more serious neighbors.

This *kulelat* syndrome was unfortunate. It made our people unsure of themselves, unduly cynical about our prospects as a nation and the ability of government or anyone to pull the country together and win a future. Perhaps without meaning to, the Pied Pipers among us have led our people to the Slough of Despond, echoing hollowly the tired tunes taught us by those who would want us to image ourselves as somewhat cracked, a "damaged culture" whose centuries of colonization has made us permanently disabled. A climate of nullity has been created, disempowering many who otherwise would have gone on doing what they need to do, believing that just ahead is the way to a future.

Mercifully, we are now brightening up as a people.[1] From the "sick man of Asia" we are now seen as "Asia's bright spot" and predicted to be one of the world's leading economies by 2050 by those who are in the business of making such forecasts. This shift in mood is remarkable in that it is largely perception.

The pendulum swings, depending on whose voice gets to dominate air and cyberspace. In the same way that there are times when we feel a false sense of exultation, an unwarranted optimism about ourselves that often degenerates into patriotic hysteria and triumphalism, there are also times when a country wallows unduly in negation. Hope gets obscured by an overwhelming sense of being thwarted by our own contradictions.

I suspect that this is more than a failure in perspective. It is in some way a function of the subtle presence of the demonic in the shaping of perception. Mephistopheles, that seductive figure of the demonic in *Faustus*, is described as a "spirit that always denies." He is the exact opposite of Jesus, in whom all our dreams and all our hopes find their "yes" (2 Cor 1:19–20). Satan is a grumpy, grouchy, gloomy churl always hissing from the background, snarling a "nay" to all possibility of goodness.

---

1. The recent survey of the Social Weather Station says eight out of ten Filipinos are optimistic about the future, sensing that we are now on the way to being a "developed" country. This is largely to the perception of a lower corruption index and increased business confidence.

A "War of Perception"

Most of us, particularly our young people, now live in a secondary environment of images constructed for us by media. The stories we most believe are no longer those we actually live, or what C. S. Lewis calls "primal history," but the myths and narratives spun for us by those in the business of appealing to the imagination to sell goods and dreams.

How often has your own experience of primitive reality been at odds with the perceptions peddled to us by media and other purveyors of propaganda?

The incongruity between barehands experience and the clouded notions that circulate in the etherized world of opinion leaders may have something to do with their peculiar susceptibility to the auto-suggestive power of what sociologists call "*groupthink*." It has been observed that intellectuals, of all people, are most vulnerable to whatever propaganda is in fashion, for the simple reason that they absorb the most amount of secondhand information. The poor, thankfully, are too busy surviving to pay attention to anything removed from the visceral and organic authenticity of everyday life.

That there is often a real lack of fit between actual and dominant perceptions of reality calls for awareness that we are engaged in a "war of perception." Our commitment to truth should include concern for discernment, and for guarding our own inner spirits from the contamination of unhealthy abstractions.

Paul tells the Christians at Corinth that however much they have been moved by certain ritual and ecstatic experiences, the fact is that they were being led astray to dumb idols (1 Cor 12:2). Their pagan lives were not without moments, religious highs that deceived them into thinking they were standing before the holy and the sacred. Similarly, it is possible to derive a great deal of aesthetic or intellectual satisfaction from media whose content ultimately subverts our ability to maintain an inner poise, this delicate equilibrium between a sense of the world as tragically disfigured and the sense that in the end, the "truth will out, and the lie rot," and goodness shall prevail and no longer wear the face of weakness.

I find reading existentialists like Albert Camus and other such bleak authors rather bruising and bracing, for instance. They grab you tight by the scruff of the neck, holding up an unflinching picture of a life destitute of God. Yet I do not wish to read them often, or similar stuff churned out by lesser talents among more postmodern novelists. This is not to edit reality.

It is to protect myself from moral and spiritual erosions caused by constant exposure to the seedy and the sordid.

Paul in Philippians 4:8 tells us to surround ourselves with life-affirming things: "Whatever is true, whatever is honorable, whatever is just, whatever is pure, whatever is lovely, whatever is gracious, if there is any excellence, if there is anything worthy of praise, *think about these things*." They are to be our constant environment, for there is enough in the world to guarantee the seepage of sewage.

Unlike God, we cannot get too close to spiritual squalor without ourselves getting defiled by the muck. There is a place for radical abstention, when called for by the demands of purity: "If your eye causes you to sin, pluck it out." It is better that we suffer sensory deprivation than that our whole body should ache with lust or the many injurious cravings induced by exposure to constant tittilations.

Also, what George Orwell calls "bad good art" is ultimately untrue. It is often aesthetically seductive of course, like the tree of the knowledge of good and evil. Eve saw that it was "a delight to the eyes," alluring enough to be desired to make one wise and sophisticated. Yet even the French poet Charles Baudelaire had an inkling that "evil comes up softly like a flower." Falsehood at its most perilous is when it is, for the most part, a "beautiful lie."

The lie is usually in the lack of proportion, in the inordinate emphasis put on certain facts as against others equally important. Integrity requires that we behold with tenacity and grit the brokenness of our world. It also insists that we admit into view those pieces that do not quite fit our picture of the world as hopelessly incapable of redemption.

Part of the difficulty of outright censorship is that there is much about what we see and hear that is true. All good propagandists know that persuasion is most effective when it has the ring of truth. Hitler's propaganda minister, Josef Goebbels, insisted that all Wermacht communiques be as accurate as possible. The devil is not averse to quoting even Scripture if it suits his purposes. Advertisers, knowing the importance of being earnest, prescribe as a rule of the game that they believe their own propaganda. Falsity does not always go with a want of sincerity.

Yet a little bit of untruth, like ugliness, has a way of wearing down the spirit. A little leaven leavens the whole lump, Jesus says. Beware, he says, of those who stage manage appearances. Pretty soon we will not know the difference between deception and image projection, subliminal manipulation and the art of managing perception and influencing opinion.

Put the Monsters at the Center

There was a time when the church and then the state dominated public space. In old oral societies, says the media theorist Harold Innis, the church's oral nature gave it an edge over other institutions of society: it lived by celebration, recital of mass, the singing of hymns and the giving and hearing of sermons.

With the invention of the Gutenberg press, a culture of literacy was shaped, with its emphasis on linearity and sequentiality.[2] Notice how in the West, it is an ingrained habit to queue for everything; there are orderly lines for buses, supermarkets, even toilets. Cities like New York are organized in straight lines, numbered in a straightforward way. Contrast this with the simultaneous movement of crowds clambering onto buses, the multi-tasking of sellers attending to a number of customers at once in wet markets, and the maze-like streets that curve and circle round and run into dead ends in many other, older parts of the world.

Sociologically, tribal leadership passed from the hands of those who were keepers of memory – the elders – to those who can read and write. In the age of secular ideologies, the state eventually edged out the church, relegating it to mumbling in corners about the meaning of its own symbols. In the crowded plasticity of a wired world, where everyone can upload stuff in cyberspace and electronic media, both the church and the state now have to compete with all sorts of consciousness industries to even gain a hearing.

Apart from needing new frames of theological meaning, the church needs new wineskins in communicating the gospel. Protestant offshoots of the Reformation, particularly, need to break out of their linear, abstract and analytical culture if they are to make sense in oral cultures or in the largely intuitive, image-laden and nonlinear culture of those used to the simultaneous images of interactive media.

We need to shift from our heavily left-brained orientation – expository sermons, inductive bible study, abstract theological discourse – to a mostly right-brained mode of presentation that puts emphasis on story rather than exposition, parable and not argumentation, imagination rather than cognition.

Perhaps more critically, the church needs to stand as a Sign to the powers that Jesus is lord over all the forces that seek to make us conform to their image of the good life. This requires the capacity to name accurately the idols of our time.

---

2. See Marshall McLuhan's famous *Understanding Media: The Extensions of Man* (Whitby, ON: McGraw-Hill, 1964).

Because things are now a little more complex and we are not exactly sure where lies the enemy, naming the powers may mean facing up to the shadows beneath the neon lights. It means refusing to get entertained and blindsided, banishing to the edges the murky things that fill us with such abstract terror.

Novelists speak of "dark liquid nights," of an ectoplasmic mist that descends upon us and fills the room with gloom and doom and a sorrow that seems unto death. On our walls we yet see the shadow of a stain, but we do not know whence it comes from or how it got there. By instinct, many sense that deep in the heart of things is a dreadful horror, but most of the time we skirt round it, accounting it to some dysfunction in the system or, as J. R. R. Tolkien once said, always suspecting it may be somehow connected with the government.

It is time we put the monsters at the center, he said. Like the hapless hobbits inching their way to Mordor to destroy the Ring of Power, we are to take the perilous journey of tracking down the Dragon to its lair, even if we fear the overwhelming power of the Harlot riding on the scarlet Beast (Rev 17).

Through the fog of people's angst and nameless dread, we are to wrestle and ferret the demonic out of the corners of our consciousness, detect and articulate its tell-tale marks, and speak a discerning Word to societies needing insight.

This prophetic discernment requires the church to nurture a poetic imagination. The practice of this, says the theologian Walter Brueggeman in his commentary on Isaiah,

> is the most subversive, redemptive act that a leader of a faith community can undertake in the midst of exile. This work of poetic alternative in the long run is more crucial than one-on-one pastoral care or the careful implementation of institutional goals. That is because the work of poetic imagination holds the potential of unleashing a community of power and action that finally will not be contained by any imperial restrictions and definitions of reality.

A powerful example of this in the New Testament is Jesus' way of teaching parables, inviting his community of listeners beyond the visible realities of Roman law and the restrictions of Jewish law. Jesus called his people to step out of tradition and venture into a specific, open-ended, alternative society called the "kingdom of God." He did not give them a fixed blueprint or a program. Instead, he turned people loose from the givens of the day and inspired them to live toward new social possibilities.[3]

This prophetic imagination requires that we be both fiercely acute and courageously kind, willing to be surprised that something so hideous may yet charm us. As the German poet Rilke has said of the things we fear: "Perhaps all the dragons of our lives are really only princesses just waiting for us to be once beautiful and brave."

Global media has successfully packaged for us a synthetic environment where all that glitters is told and nothing much is said about the quiet, homely gestures that quicken belief in the invincibility of goodness. There are no cameras clicking for the act of giving a cup of water to the thirsty. Yet it is gestures like these which make up our *primal history* – the all-important story of how lives which are hid in Christ are bringing about a new order of things.

Meanwhile, it pays to know when the prince of the power of the air is "on air" and puts on a show. If you're like me, I merely turn off the TV or radio and go back to dreaming and smelling the steaming mist of goodness rising like a tempest out of my morning cup of coffee.

---

3. Brueggemann, *Hopeful Imagination*, 96–97.

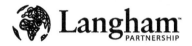 **Langham**
PARTNERSHIP

Langham Literature and its imprints are a ministry of Langham Partnership.

Langham Partnership is a global fellowship working in pursuit of the vision God entrusted to its founder John Stott –

> *to facilitate the growth of the church in maturity and Christ-likeness through raising the standards of biblical preaching and teaching.*

Our vision is to see churches in the majority world equipped for mission and growing to maturity in Christ through the ministry of pastors and leaders who believe, teach and live by the Word of God.

Our mission is to strengthen the ministry of the Word of God through:
- nurturing national movements for biblical preaching
- fostering the creation and distribution of evangelical literature
- enhancing evangelical theological education

especially in countries where churches are under-resourced.

Our ministry

Langham Preaching partners with national leaders to nurture indigenous biblical preaching movements for pastors and lay preachers all around the world. With the support of a team of trainers from many countries, a multi-level programme of seminars provides practical training, and is followed by a programme for training local facilitators. Local preachers' groups and national and regional networks ensure continuity and ongoing development, seeking to build vigorous movements committed to Bible exposition.

Langham Literature provides majority world preachers, scholars and seminary libraries with evangelical books and electronic resources through publishing and distribution, grants and discounts. The programme also fosters the creation of indigenous evangelical books in many languages, through writer's grants, strengthening local evangelical publishing houses, and investment in major regional literature projects, such as one volume Bible commentaries like *The Africa Bible Commentary* and *The South Asia Bible Commentary*.

Langham Scholars provides financial support for evangelical doctoral students from the majority world so that, when they return home, they may train pastors and other Christian leaders with sound, biblical and theological teaching. This programme equips those who equip others. Langham Scholars also works in partnership with majority world seminaries in strengthening evangelical theological education. A growing number of Langham Scholars study in high quality doctoral programmes in the majority world itself. As well as teaching the next generation of pastors, graduated Langham Scholars exercise significant influence through their writing and leadership.

To learn more about Langham Partnership and the work we do visit **langham.org**

Wenham, Gordon J. "Laws and Ethical Ideals in Deuteronomy." In *For Our Good Always: Studies on the Message and Influence of Deuteronomy in Honor of Daniel I. Block*, edited by Jason S. De Rouchie, Jason Gile, and Kenneth J. Turner. Winona Lake, IN: Eisenbrauns, 2013.

Westermann, Claus. *Genesis 1–11: A Commentary*. Translated by John J. Scullion. Minneapolis, MN: Augsburg Publishing House, 1984 (first published 1974).

Wright, Christopher J. H. *Walking in the Ways of the Lord: The Ethical Authority of the OT*. Downers Grove, IL: InterVarsity, 1995.

Wright, N. T. *Acts for Everyone, Part One*. London: SPCK /Louisville, KY: John Knox Press, 2008.

Yeo, K. K. *Navigating Romans through Cultures: Challenging Readings by Charting a New Course*. Romans through History and Culture Series. New York: T & T Clark, 2004.

Mouw, Richard J. *When the Kings Come Marching In.* Grand Rapids, MI: Eerdmans, 1983.

Ortney, Sherry B. "Is Female to Male as Nature Is to Culture?" In *Women, Culture and Society,* edited by Michelle Zimbalist Rosaldo and Louise Lamphere. Stanford, CA: Stanford University Press, 1974.

Ramachandra, Vinoth. *Subverting Global Myths: Theology and the Public Issues Shaping Our World.* Downers Grove, IL: InterVarsity, 2008.

Rius-Camps, Josep, and Jenny Read-Heimerdinger, eds. *The Message of Acts in Codex Bezae: A Comparison with the Alexandrian Tradition Vol II, Acts 6:1–12.25.* Library of New Testament Studies, 302. New York/London: T & T Clark, 2006.

————, eds. *The Message of Acts in Codex Bezae: A Comparison with the Alexandrian Tradition Vol III, Acts 13.1–18.23, The Ends of the Earth.* Library of New Testament Studies, 365. New York/London: T & T Clark, 2007.

Santos, Narry. "Tagapamagitan: A Cultural Bridge for Loving the Sojourner." In *The Gospel in Culture: Contextualization Issues through Asian Eyes,* edited by Melba Padilla Maggay. Mandaluyong, Metro Manila: OMFLiterature, 2013.

Sparks, Kenton L. *Ethnicity and Identity in Ancient Israel: Prolegomena to the Study of Ethnic Sentiments and their Expression in the Hebrew Bible.* Winona Lake, IN: Eisenbrauns, 1998.

Stanley, Tim, and Alexander Lee. "It's Still Not the End of History." *The Atlantic,* 1 September 2014.

Stark, Rodney. *How the West Won: The Neglected Story of the Triumph of Modernity.* Wilmington, DE: ISI Books, 2014.

Stendahl, Krister. "The Apostle Paul and the Introspective Conscience of the West." *HTR* 56 (1963).

Swartley, Willard. *Slavery, Sabbath, War and Women: Case Studies in Biblical Interpretations.* Scottdale, PA: Herald Press, 1983.

Tehranian, Majid, and Katharine Kia. "That Recurrent Suspicion: Democratization in a Global Perspective." In *The Democratization of Communication,* edited by Philip Lee. Cardiff: University of Wales Press, 1995.

Turner, Kenneth J. "Deuteronomy's Theology of Exile." In *For Our Good Always: Studies on the Message and Influence of Deuteronomy in Honor of Daniel I. Block,* edited by Jason S. De Rouchie, Jason Gile, and Kenneth J. Turner. Winona Lake, IN: Eisenbrauns, 2013.

Turner, Laurence A. *Genesis, Readings: A New Biblical Commentary.* Sheffield: Sheffield Academic Press, 2009.

von Rad, Gerhard. *Genesis: A Commentary,* revised edition. Philadelphia, PA: The Westminster Press, 1972.

Walls, Andrew F. *The Missionary Movement in Christian History: Studies in the Transmission of the Faith.* Maryknoll, NY: Orbis Books, 1996.

Geertz, C. *The Interpretation of Cultures*. New York: Basic Books, 1973.

Gill, John. *Genesis*. Newport Bible Commentary. Springfield, MO: Particular Baptist Press, 2010. (First published as *Volume One, An Exposition of the Old Testament*. London: Aaron Ward.)

Griffiths, Valerie. "Mankind Male and Female." In *The Role of Women (When Christians Disagree)*, edited by Shirley Lees. Leicester: IVP, 1984.

Habel, Norman. *The Birth, the Curse and the Greening of Earth: An Ecological Reading of Genesis 1–11*. Sheffield: Sheffield Phoenix Press, 2011.

Hall, Edward T. *Beyond Culture*. Garden City, NY: Anchor Press, 1976.

Hurley, James. "1 Corinthians." In *Man and Woman in Biblical Perspective*. Leicester: IVP, 1981.

Kaiser, Walter. *Toward Old Testament Ethics*. Grand Rapids, MI: Zondervan, 1983.

Keil, C. F., and F. Delitzsch, eds. *The Pentateuch Vol 1. Commentary on the Old Testament in Ten Volumes*. Translated from German by James Martin. Grand Rapids, MI: Eerdmans, 1981.

Kessler, Martin, and Karel Deurloo. *A Commentary on Genesis: The Book of Beginnings*. Mahwah, NJ: Paulist Press International, 2004.

Kevan, E. F. "Genesis." In *The New Bible Commentary*, edited by F. Davidson. Leicester: IVP, 1965.

Kirk, Andrew. "Theology from a Feminist Perspective." In *Men, Women and God*, edited by Kathy Keay. Basingstoke: Marshall Pickering, 1987.

Knauth, R. J. D. "Alien, Foreign Resident." In *Dictionary of the OT Pentateuch*, edited by T. Desmond Alexander and David W. Baker. Downers Grove, IL: InterVarsity, 2003.

Maggay, Melba Padilla. *A Clash of Cultures: Early American Protestant Missions and Filipino Religious Consciousness*. Mandaluyong City: De La Salle University Press and Anvil Publishing, 2011.

———. "Communicating the Gospel from Within, Some Culture Themes." In *Doing Theology in the Philippines*, edited by John Suk. Mandaluyong: OMFLit, 2005.

———. *Rise Up and Walk: Religion and Culture in Empowering the Poor*. Oxford: Regnum, 2016.

Maly, Eugene H. "Genesis." In *The Jerome Biblical Commentary*, edited by Raymond E. Brown, Joseph A. Fitzmyer, and Roland E. Murphy. Englewood Cliffs, NJ: Prentice-Hall, 1968.

Mander, Jerry, and Edward Goldsmith, eds. *The Case against the Global Economy, and a Turn toward the Local*. San Francisco, CA: Sierra Club Books, 1996.

Mangahas, Fe, and Jenny Romero-Llaguno. *Centennial Crossings: Readings in Babaylan Feminism in the Philippines*. Quezon City: C and E Publishing, 2006.

McLuhan, Marshall. *Understanding Media: The Extensions of Man*. Whitby, ON: McGraw-Hill, 1964.

Bibliography

Anderson, Bernhard. *From Creation to New Creation.* Minneapolis, MN: Fortress Press, 1994.

Bandstra, Barry L. *Reading the Old Testament: An Introduction to the Hebrew Bible,* 2nd ed. Belmont, CA: Wadsworth, 1999.

Berger, Peter, ed. *The Desecularization of the World: Resurgent Religion and World Politics.* Washington, DC: Ethics and Public Policy Center; Grand Rapids, MI: Eerdmans, 1999.

Block, D. I. "Sojourner, Alien, Stranger." In *The International Standard Bible Enclopedia,* vol. 4, edited by Geoffrey W. Bromiley. Grand Rapids, MI: Eerdmans, 1982.

Brueggemann, Walter. *A Commentary on Jeremiah: Exile and Homecoming.* Grand Rapids, MI: Eerdmans, 1998.

———. *Hopeful Imagination: Prophetic Voices in Exile.* Philadelphia, PA: Fortress Press, 1986.

———. *The Land: Place as Gift, Promise and Challenge in Biblical Faith,* 2nd edition. Overtures to Biblical Theology. Minneapolis, MN: Fortress, 2002.

———. "A Shattered Transcendence? Exile and Restoration," In *Biblical Theology: Problems and Perspectives: In Honor of J. Christiaan Becker,* edited by J. C. Beker, S. J. Kraftchick, C. D. Myers, and B. C. Ollenburger. Nashville, TN: Abingdon, 1995.

Cassuto, Umberto. *A Commentary on the Book of Genesis,* Part 2. Jerusalem: Magnes Press, 1964.

Cawley, F. "Jeremiah." *The New Bible Commentary.* Edited by F. Davidson. Leicester: IVP, 1965.

Curtis, E. M. "Images in Mesopotamia and the Bible: A Comparative Study." In *The Bible in the Light of Cuneiform Literature. Scripture in Context III,* Ancient Near Eastern Texts and Studies, edited by W. W. Hallo, B. W. Jones, and G. L. Mattingly, 31–56. Lewiston, NY: Edwin Mellen, 1990.

de Mesa, Jose M. "Hispanic Catholicism and Lowland Filipino Culture." *ISACC Research on Early Protestant Missions and the Indigenous Consciousness, Track 2, Conversion to Protestant Christianity Report, Vol. II,* 3.

Delitzsch, Franz. *A New Commentary on Genesis,* Vol. 1. Grand Rapids, MI: Eerdmans, 1951.

Ellul, Jacques. *The Meaning of the City.* Translated by Dennis Pardee. Grand Rapids, MI: Eerdmans, 1970; Carlisle: Paternoster, 1997.

Endō, Shūsaku. *Silence.* New York: Taplinger, 1979 (first published in 1966).

Fukuyuma, Francis. "The End of History?" *The National Interest,* Summer 1989.

Lightning Source UK Ltd.
Milton Keynes UK
UKOW05f1326280317
297719UK00001B/3/P